STITCH

STITCH

20 EMBROIDERY MAKES FOR YOUR HOME & WARDROBE

AMY BURT

CONTENTS

INTRODUCTION

Traditional hand embroidery has been used for centuries as a means of expression, but it often evokes images that are old-fashioned and stuffy and these stereotypes can be hard to shake off. However, modern embroidery is used as a voice to deliver strong and defiant messages in any language around the world. Today, this voice is more important and relevant than ever.

Almost anyone can pick up a needle and thread and make a mark on a piece of fabric that is 100% personal and unique. In this book, I will introduce you to a range of projects aimed at complete beginners. The projects each have a difficulty rating, ranging from 1–3, allowing you to progress as you gain experience.

The stitches are shown in the Stitch Directory, which you will find in the Know How chapter at the back of the book. Once you have learnt the stitches, you will be able to put them to use in a variety of ways on a multitude of projects; I have simply shown examples of what can be achieved on items easily found at home. In the Know How chapter you will also find all the basic techniques and advice on what you will need to have in your embroidery kit.

I hope this book inspires you to try many of the projects, and you go on to create your own unique embroidered designs.

>>> EYES GLASSES CASE

Transform a plain glasses case into an eye-catching accessory with this super-cool design that uses a simple chain stitch.

✖ Find the Eyes template on page 116

YOU WILL NEED
Soft glasses case (this one is made of felt)
Embroidery scissors
Tweezers
Embroidery transfer paper
Craft scissors
Ballpoint pen
Fabric pen
Embroidery needle, size 7–10
Black stranded cotton
Tapestry needle, size 26
Machine thread (the same colour as the case)

STITCHES
Double running stitch (see page 106)
Chain stitch (see page 108)

NOTE
Use a standard 16in (40cm) length of thread throughout.

Tip

You will need a glasses case that is easy to get your hand inside for stitching, or simple to take apart then reassemble.

STEP 1

Use embroidery scissors to unpick the stitching on the glasses case until it can be opened out flat. This will enable you to embroider it more easily. Take care not to cut the fabric when unpicking the stitches; using tweezers will help.

STEP 2

Trace the Eyes template onto a piece of embroidery transfer paper (see page 100). Trim the paper down to a manageable size with craft scissors. With the powdery side of the paper face down on the glasses case, draw over the design with a ballpoint pen. Make sure you press hard with the pen and go over the lines several times.

STEP 3

Remove the embroidery transfer paper, then draw over the transfer lines with a fabric pen.

STEP 4

Thread the embroidery needle with three strands of black stranded cotton. Use the stab-stitch method (see page 104) to secure your thread, then work a row of chain stitch along each design line. Try to work the stitches quite small – approximately $5/64$–$1/8$in (2–3mm) long – keeping the size and tension consistent. When you have run out of thread, secure it using the stab-stitch method or, if there is no room for stab stitches, weave the thread along the back of the stitches (see page 104).

Tip

When using multiple strands of cotton in the needle, take care to ensure the strands lie even and smooth as you stitch.

STEP 5

When you reach the eyelashes, make sure to work each lash in the same direction – from top to bottom. Avoid trailing long threads across the reverse, as the threads can get caught up and damaged; instead, weave the thread along the reverse of the stitches.

STEP 6

Continue the same process for the rest of the design.

STEP 7

For the centre of the eye, work continuous rows of chain stitch, closely together in a spiral formation. Make sure that none of the fabric is showing too much.

Tip

Work the rows of stitches closer together than you may think necessary.

STEP 8

When the embroidery is complete, you will need to sew the case back together. I have used a double running stitch because it looks the same from the front as it does from the back. Use a machine thread in the same colour as the case and a tapestry needle. The tapestry needle, being blunt, will ensure you go through the same holes as the original stitches. A sharp embroidery needle is more likely to create a new hole. To start and finish the running stitch, go over the first and last stitch three times, then take the thread to the inside of the case and cut.

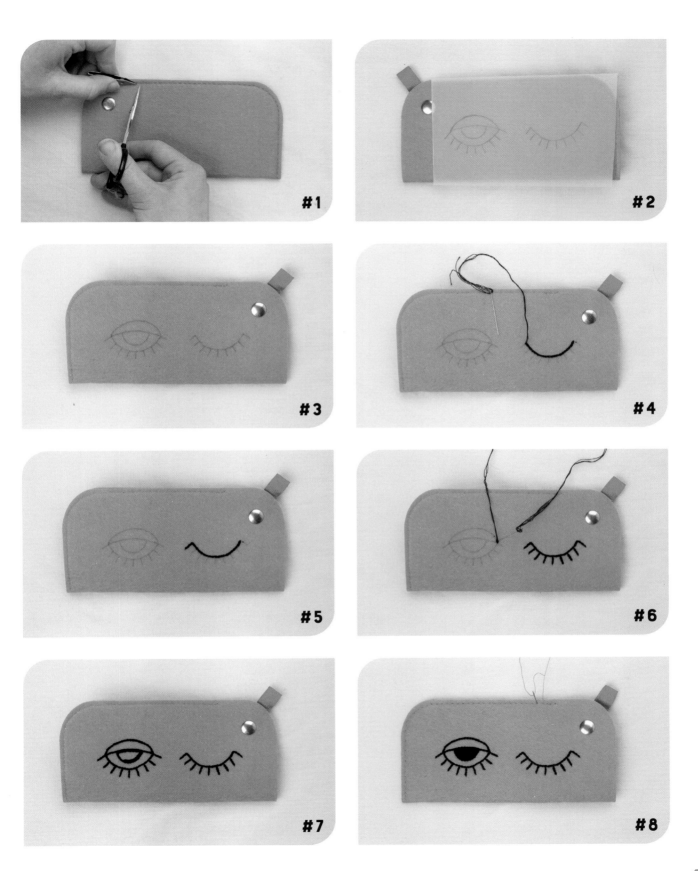

#1

#2

#3

#4

#5

#6

#7

#8

≫ ANCHOR TOP

Give a nautical twist to a classic striped top. This anchor design uses couching and stem stitch in stranded cottons.

✖ Find the Anchor template on page 116

YOU WILL NEED
Thin tracing paper
Striped top
Pins
Embroidery transfer paper
Ballpoint pen
Water-soluble fabric pens in two different colours
    (to show up on the stripes)
Embroidery hoop, measuring at least 4in (10cm)
Tear-away embroidery stabilizer
Embroidery scissors
Embroidery needles, sizes 7 and 10
Machine thread for tacking (in contrasting colour)
Chenille needle, size 22–24
Stranded cotton in grey and yellow
    (the one used here has a metallic mix)
Cotton bud
Iron

STITCHES
Running stitch (see page 106)
Backstitch (see page 106)
Stem stitch (see page 107)
Couching (see page 115)

Tip

It may help to put a book inside the top to provide a hard surface on which to draw.

NOTE
Use a standard 16in (40cm) length of thread unless otherwise stated.

STEP 1

Start by tracing the anchor template onto thin tracing paper, then decide where on your top you would like it placed. Mark this area with pins.

STEP 2

Take the embroidery transfer paper and place it face down onto the top. Place the tracing of the design over the carbon paper and draw firmly over the design with a ballpoint pen.

STEP 3

Carefully take away the embroidery transfer paper and the design should be lightly revealed on the top. Draw over the design with a combination of the two water-soluble pens, so that it is clearly visible on each stripe.

STEP 4

Place a small embroidery hoop over the design. Now cut a rectangle of the tear-away embroidery stabilizer that is just bigger than the anchor.

STEP 5

Using contrasting machine thread and a size 10 embroidery needle, tack the stabilizer to the reverse of the top using a large running stitch.

NOTE: Stabilizer is needed when working on fabric with a slight stretch to prevent it from distorting.

STEP 6

Returning to the front of the design, take a long length – approximately 32in (80cm) – of all six strands of yellow thread. Thread them through the chenille needle so that the are tied doubled over and become approximately 16in (40cm) long. At the bottom curve of the anchor, carefully secure the thread using the stab-stitch method (see page 104). Now thread two strands of the yellow thread through a size 10 embroidery needle. Make two backstitches at the tip of the curve in an arrow style.

STEP 7

Holding the thick yellow thread over the design line, couch it down with the thinner yellow thread.

STEP 8

Continue to couch the base of the anchor, not forgetting to stitch the arrow at the opposite end. When you have reached the end, weave the thick thread along the stitches on the reverse of the work (see page 104). Bring it up again at the centre of the base and continue to couch the thick thread down over the rest of the shape. Secure the thread on the reverse of the work, ensuring there are no loose threads.

STEP 9

Using a size 7 embroidery needle, thread three strands of grey stranded cotton. Secure the thread at the base of the line using the stab-stitch method and neatly work a single row of stem stitch up the design line. Leave a gap so that the stitches appear to go behind the anchor. Take care not to disturb the yellow thread when working over the anchor.

STEP 10

Secure the grey thread on the reverse of the work by weaving through the stitches and remove the tacking thread around the stabilizer. You can now tear away the stabilizer, leaving a border around the stitches. Make sure there are no sharp edges on the stabilizer, so that it's comfortable against the skin.

STEP 11

To finish, gently clean away the design lines with a damp cotton bud and press the top with an iron set on a medium heat to remove the hoop mark.

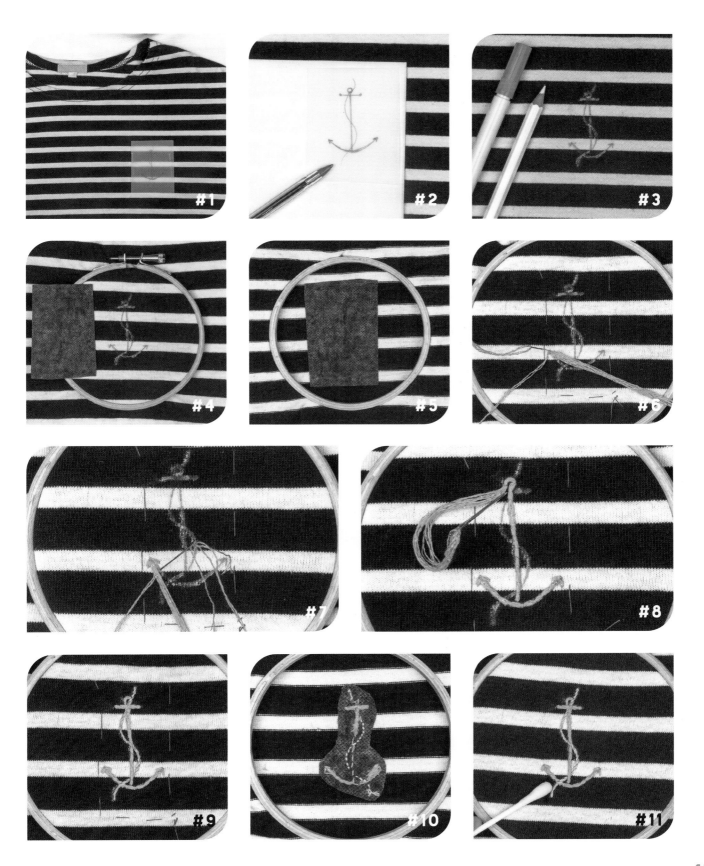

LIGHTNING-STRIKE SNEAKERS

Update a plain pair of sneakers with a lightning-strike motif worked in laid stitch and backstitch using Perle cottons.

✳ Find the Lightning-strike template on page 117

YOU WILL NEED
Heavy-weight tracing paper or a photocopier
Pencil
Craft scissors
Canvas sneakers
Pins
Fine-tipped water-soluble fabric pen
Ruler
Embroidery needle, size 5–7
Embroidery scissors
Strong thread, e.g. Perle or Coton a Broder, in yellow, orange and white
Cotton bud

STITCHES
Backstitch (see page 106)
Laid stitch (see page 113)

NOTE
Use a standard 16in (40cm) length of thread throughout.

STEP 1

Start by tracing the template onto a heavy-weight tracing paper, or photocopying it onto heavy paper. Cut the template out and pin it to the outer side of one of the sneakers. Assess its position. Move it around until you are happy.

STEP 2

Carefully draw around the template with a fine-tipped water-soluble fabric pen. Using a ruler will help to ensure you get crisp lines. (Make sure the ruler is clean, so you don't get dirty marks on your sneakers.)

STEP 3

Thread a length of yellow thread through the embroidery needle. Secure the thread in the middle of the lightning strike using the stab-stitch method (see page 104).

STEP 4

Work a diagonal in laid stitch, as shown, and bring your needle back up again next to where you took the last stitch down.

NOTE: There should never be any threads travelling along the back when you work laid stitch.

STEP 5

Work one half of the lightning strike at a time, making sure that the angle of the lightning strike stays sharp and none of the threads overlap. When you reach the tip, take the thread to the reverse and finish off the thread by catching the lining a few times.

STEP 6

Work the other half of the lightning strike in the same way. Then, thread a length of orange thread through the embroidery needle and secure it in the middle of the lightning strike using the stab-stitch method.

STEP 7

Work a single row of backstitch close to the yellow laid stitch.

STEP 8

Work three lines of backstitch as shown.

STEP 9

The laid stitch now needs securing down, otherwise the stitches might move. On the reverse of the design, secure a new strand of white thread by weaving through the stitches (see page 104), then work a tiny row of backstitch down the centre of the top and bottom parts of the lightning strike. Avoid trailing threads along the back of the work, as these could break when you are wearing the sneaker; instead, try travelling the thread inside the lining. When all the embroidery is complete, dip a cotton bud in water and gently dab away any of the visible pen lines.

STEP 10

Repeat the same process on the other sneaker, remembering to reverse the lightning strike.

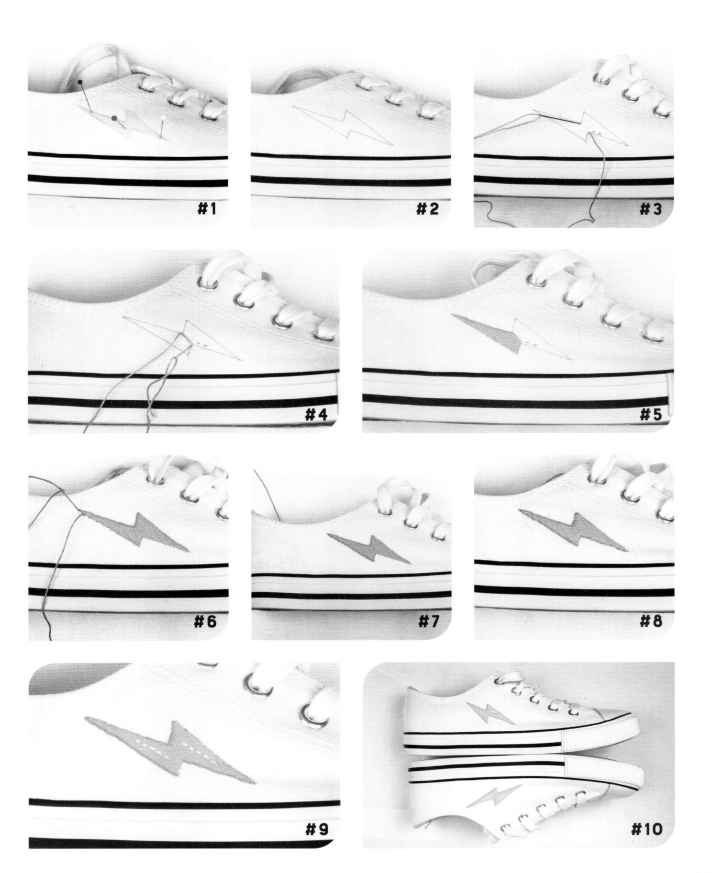

>>> RAINBOW JEANS

Brighten up an old pair of jeans with a bold, colourful rainbow design using strong split stitch and tapestry wool.

✖ Use a protractor, or a similar curved shape, as a template

YOU WILL NEED
Jeans (ideally non-stretch)
Water-soluble fabric pen
Small embroidery hoop, measuring 4–6in (10–15cm)
Tear-away embroidery stabilizer
    (if your jeans are made of stretch denim)
Chenille needle, size 22
Tapestry wool in purple, dark blue, pale blue,
    green, yellow, pink and red
Iron

STITCHES
Split stitch (see page 107)

NOTE
Use a standard 16in (40cm) length of thread throughout.

STEP 1

Choose which pocket you would like to embroider and gather your threads together. Take a curved shape, such as a protractor, to use as a template to draw the inner curve of the rainbow.

Tip

If you do not want to go through the pocket AND the jeans, you can carefully detach the pocket by cutting away the stitches from the reverse, then reattaching it after it has been embroidered.

STEP 2

Draw the curve onto the pocket using a water-soluble fabric pen. Place an embroidery hoop over the curve, ensuring the fabric is taut.

NOTE: If you are working on stretch denim, take care not to overstretch the material. Use embroidery stabilizer to reinforce your work.

STEP 3

Thread a chenille needle with a length of purple tapestry wool. Secure the thread using the stab-stitch method (see page 104) at the base of the curve. Begin to split stitch. Make each stitch approximately $^1/_8 - ^5/_{32}$in (3–4mm) long.

STEP 4

Take the needle back up through the centre of the first stitch, making sure it is evenly split.

STEP 5

Work the split stitch all the way to the end of the curve, securing the thread off next to the last stitch using the stab-stitch method.

STEP 6

Repeat another row of purple split stitch, making sure you start at the bottom of the rainbow.

STEP 7

Repeat the same process for every colour, working two rows of each one and always in the same direction. This rainbow is worked: purple, dark blue, pale blue, green, yellow, pink and red. You can add or take away colours of your choice. Secure your last thread along the back, running the thread through the reverse of the stitches (see page 104).

STEP 8

To finish, remove the hoop and gently press the jeans from the reverse with an iron.

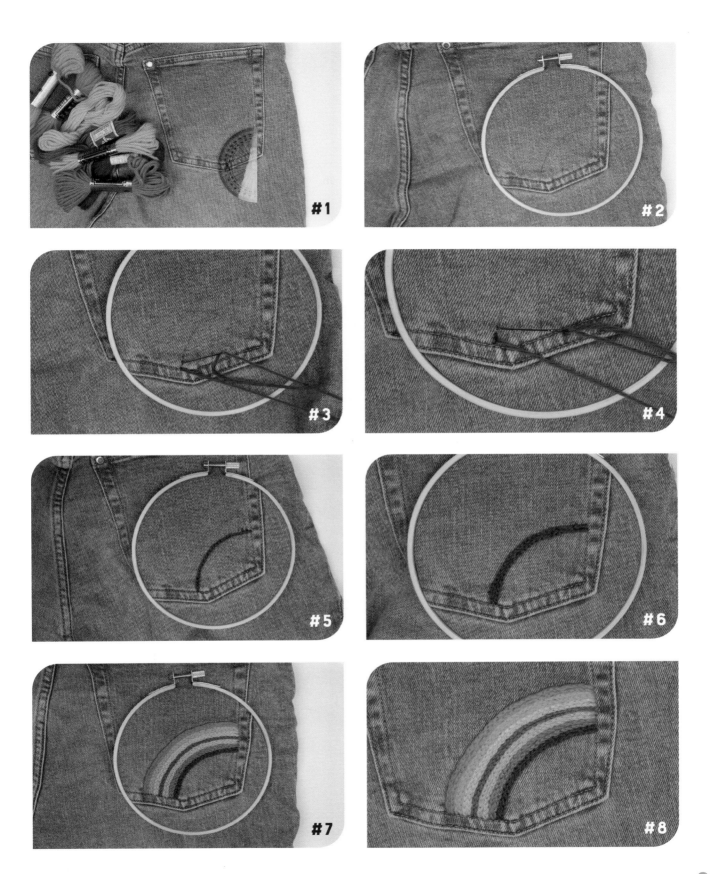

⟫⟫ CACTI CUSHION

Create a statement cushion with this sunset-coloured cacti design worked in tactile French knots.

✖ Find the Cacti template on page 117

YOU WILL NEED

Large sheet of tissue paper
Blue coloured pencil
Cushion cover
Large embroidery hoop (size dependent on cushion)
Pins
Embroidery needle, size 10
Embroidery scissors
Machine thread in pale blue
Tweezers (optional)
Tapestry needle, size 22–24
Chenille needle, size 24
Tapestry wool in yellow, orange, pink, lilac and pale blue
Iron
Small embroidery hoop, measuring 6in (15cm)

STITCHES

Running stitch (see page 106)
French knots (see page 115)

NOTE
Use a standard 16in (40cm) length of thread throughout.

STEP 1

Start by tracing the Cacti template onto a large sheet of tissue paper using a blue coloured pencil (blue is a colour that will not show up if it is accidentally transferred onto the cushion cover).

STEP 2

Take the cushion cover and place a large embroidery hoop over the main area you will be working. Pin the tissue paper into place, making sure your pins are clean.

STEP 3

Thread the embroidery needle with a length of pale-blue machine cotton. Starting in the middle of the design, begin a large running stitch.

NOTE: Do not secure your thread too tightly to start, as it will be removed at the end of the project; simply go over the first stitch three times.

STEP 4

Work the running stitch using a long stitch on the top and a short thread underneath. Stitches should be approximately $^{13}/_{64}$–$^{3}/_{8}$in (5–10mm) long.

STEP 5

When you have covered all the blue pencil lines with running stitch, carefully rip away the tissue paper. Use tweezers or a tapestry needle to remove any small pieces that remain. You will be left with the outline of the two cacti in pale-blue running stitch.

STEP 6

Thread the chenille needle with yellow tapestry wool. Secure the thread at the centre bottom of the design, between the two cacti, using the stab-stitch method (see page 104). (Make sure these stitches are eventually covered.) Start to work a scattered arrangement of French knots.

STEP 7

When you have used up the first length of yellow wool, end your thread with the stab-stitch method. Change to orange thread and work around the yellow French knots. Work the knots closely together near the cacti and slightly more spread apart as you get farther away.

Tip

You can always add more yellow French knots to the design at a later stage, or revisit any other previously worked colours.

STEP 8

After the orange thread you can start to use the pink. When you feel you are in an area that needs to change colour, work the French knots farther apart to give the impression of blending into the next colour.

Tip

If you have no place to stab stitch when ending and starting a thread, you can secure the threads on the reverse by tying on to the back of the previously worked stitches.

STEP 9

Continue the same method with the lilac thread, then work in the pale blue. The pale blue will be much more spread out than the previous colours.

STEP 10

When there is no more room on the hoop to work, take the hoop off and press the creases away with an iron set to a medium heat. You can now use a small embroidery hoop to work the scattered French knots on the rest of the cushion.

Tip

Take care when travelling your thread along the back. If it is too tight it will pucker the fabric.

STEP 11

When you are happy that the design is complete, carefully remove the pale-blue tacking thread. Gently turn the cushion cover inside out and press with a medium/cool iron.

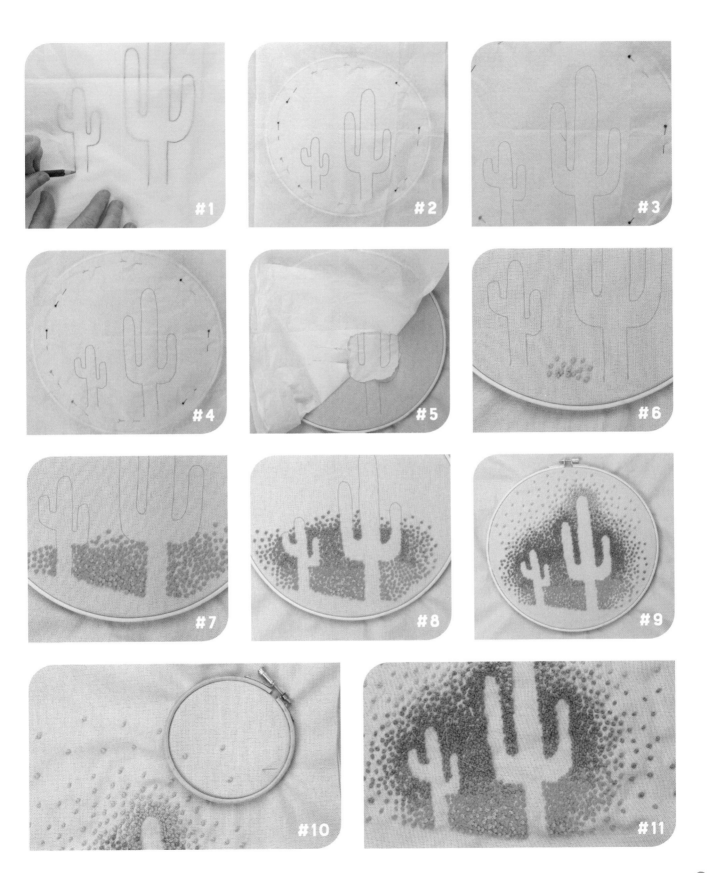

MEXICAN-SKULL SWEATSHIRT

Create a dazzling impact with this Mexican-inspired skull. It uses satin stitch over padding with gold metallic threads and details in black stranded cotton.

✖ Find the Mexican-skull template on page 118

YOU WILL NEED
Firm, non-adhesive interfacing
Fine-tipped water-soluble fabric pen
Embroidery scissors
Sweatshirt
Pins
Small embroidery hoop, measuring 6–8in (15–20cm)
Tear-away embroidery stabilizer (optional)
Embroidery needle, size 7–10
Machine thread (for tacking)
Metallic gold embroidery thread
Black stranded cotton
Iron

STITCHES
Running stitch (see page 106)
Backstitch (see page 106)
Lazy daisy (detached chain stitch) (see page 108)
Satin stitch (see page 112)

NOTE
Use a standard 16in (40cm) length of thread throughout.

STEP 1

Take the Mexican-skull template and place a piece of firm, non-adhesive interfacing on top, so that you can see the design through it. Trace the main outlines of the skull onto the interfacing with a water-soluble fabric pen.

STEP 2

Cut out the template, including the eyes and nostrils. Decide where you would like to place the skull on the sweatshirt then pin it into place. Lay a small embroidery hoop over the area.

NOTE: If you are embroidering a stretchy fabric, apply a tear-away embroidery stabilizer to the back, to strengthen your embroidery.

STEP 3

Thread the embroidery needle with a length of machine cotton. Work several rows of running stitch down the centre of the skull and two rows to form an 'X'. Make sure you do not secure the thread tightly, as you will need to remove it when you work over it later.

STEP 4

Thread the embroidery needle with two strands of gold metallic thread. Secure the thread using the stab-stitch method (see page 104), angled underneath the interfacing. Starting in the middle of the skull, begin to work the satin stitch. Try to work the stitch at a 45-degree angle. If working the bottom half of the skull first, work the stitch in an upwards direction.

STEP 5

Continue to work the bottom half of the skull in sections, ensuring you angle the needle 'around' the interfacing to create a smooth edge.

STEP 6

When the entire lower half is complete, begin to work the top half of the skull, making sure you change the direction of the stitch by bringing your needle out on the opposite edge that you have just been working. Stitches must now be worked in a downwards direction. If you find your stitches are 'rolling off' the edges of the interfacing you can create a secure stitch line by working a small single running stitch 90 degrees over the satin stitches. Take the needle out of the fabric and down into the interfacing.

STEP 7

Now thread the embroidery needle with a single strand of black stranded cotton. Secure the thread from the reverse by weaving through the stitches (see page 104), then work a single row of backstitch for the mouth. Next, work single stitches over the row of backstitch to create teeth. As you do this, try to avoid moving the metallic thread too much.

STEP 8

Start a new strand of black stranded cotton and work a half lazy daisy stitch, coming over the edge of the eyes and down into the interfacing. Start each stitch approximately $5/64–1/8$in (2–3mm) away from the previous stitch. Continue for both eyes.

STEP 9

Now work the eyebrows in a single row of backstitch with three lazy daisy stitches. The heart is worked in a single row of backstitch.

Tip

The details can be worked by eye, but if you are unsure of the stitch placement then you can use the tissue paper transfer method shown on page 99.

STEP 10

To finish, work a row of lazy daisies around the outer top half of the skull in a single strand of black stranded cotton. Remove the hoop and press away any creases with an iron. If you used embroidery stabilizer, remove any excess from the reverse.

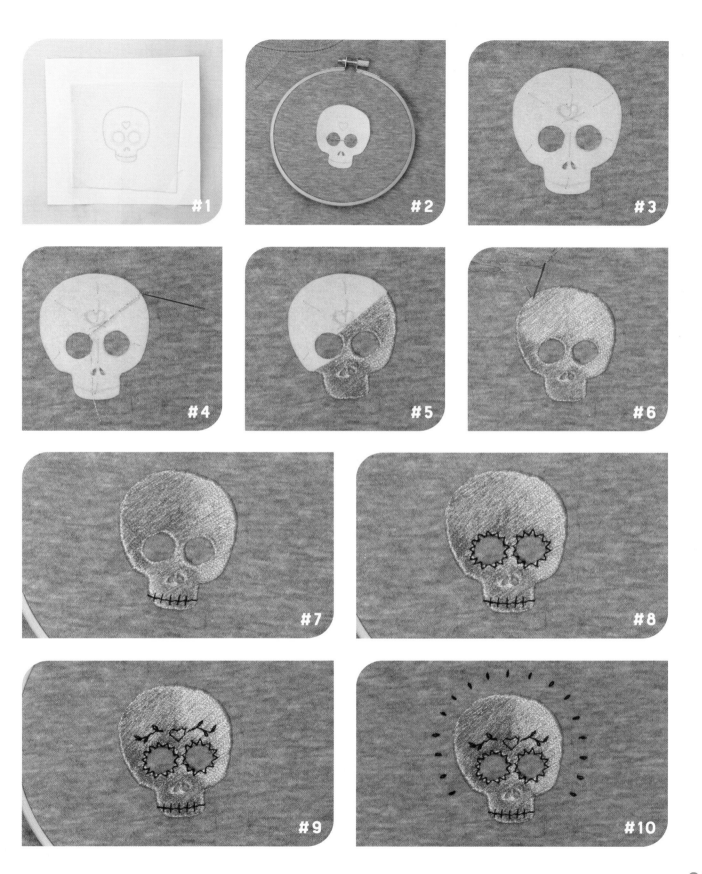

>>> LOVE-HEART BLOUSE

Wear your heart on your shirt collar with this romantic motif worked in long-and-short stitch and split stitch.

✖ Find the Love-heart template on page 118

YOU WILL NEED
Shirt or blouse
Thick paper
Craft scissors
Fine-tipped water-soluble fabric pen
Ruler
Tear-away embroidery stabilizer (optional)
Pins
Machine thread in contrasting colour
Embroidery scissors
Embroidery needle, size 8–10
Stranded cottons in red, white and black

STITCHES
Running stitch (see page 106)
Backstitch (see page 106)
Split stitch (see page 107)
Long-and-short stitch (see page 114)

NOTE
Use a standard 16in (40cm) length of thread throughout.

STEP 1

Start by tracing the love-heart template onto thick paper. Cut out the template and place it onto the left-hand collar.

STEP 2

Make sure you are happy with the placement, then carefully draw around it with a fine-tipped water-soluble fabric pen. Now draw the arrow on the other collar, using a ruler to achieve nice straight edges.

STEP 3

Some shirt collars have an interfacing; if yours doesn't, you will need to stabilize the reverse. If so, cut a small piece of tear-away embroidery stabilizer a little larger than the heart, pin it in place, then use machine cotton to tack (running stitch) it on. These stitches will be removed after the heart is complete, so use a slightly contrasting colour of machine thread to enable you to see them against the fabric.

STEP 4

Thread the embroidery needle with two strands of red stranded cotton and secure the thread on the heart outline using the stab-stitch method (see page 104). Stitch a small, tight row of split stitch all the way around the heart. Make sure the stitches are very small – approximately $5/64$in (2mm) long – to give a smooth edge for your long-and-short stitches. Finish the thread with the stab-stitch method.

STEP 5

Start up a new double strand of the red cotton, securing the thread with stab stitch, then begin the long-and-short stitch. The stitches should always be worked at the same vertical angle from the centre out; this will ensure the angle stays true. The first row of stitches must start at the lower centre of the heart and be approximately $13/64$in (5mm) long. Take the stitch over and under the split stitch.

NOTE: When working long-and-short stitch you must always split the previous stitches from the reverse and work upwards. After the first row, all stitches are worked from bottom to top. Keep where you split the stitches varied to avoid any obvious lumps and patterns. The point of long-and-short stitch is to create a smooth appearance.

Tip

If you have no place to stab stitch when ending and starting a thread, you can secure the threads on the reverse by weaving into the back of the previously worked stitches (see page 104).

STEP 6

The last long-and-short stitches must be taken over and under the split stitch so that none are visible. Make sure your stitches remain straight and you have smooth edges.

STEP 7

To make the small highlight on the heart, use two strands of white stranded cotton and secure the thread along the reverse of the heart. Work several rows of backstitch closely together in small curved lines. Once complete, you can remove the tacking stitches holding the stabilizer in place and any excess backing.

STEP 8

Now move on to the arrow design. Thread an embroidery needle with two strands of black stranded cotton. Start with the arrow head. Secure the thread within the design line using the stab-stitch method and work a small, neat row of split stitch over the design lines, working inwards to fill the centre. The stitches should be approximately $5/64 - 1/8$in (2–3mm) long.

STEP 9

To finish, work the rest of the arrow using a single row of split stitch over all the design lines.

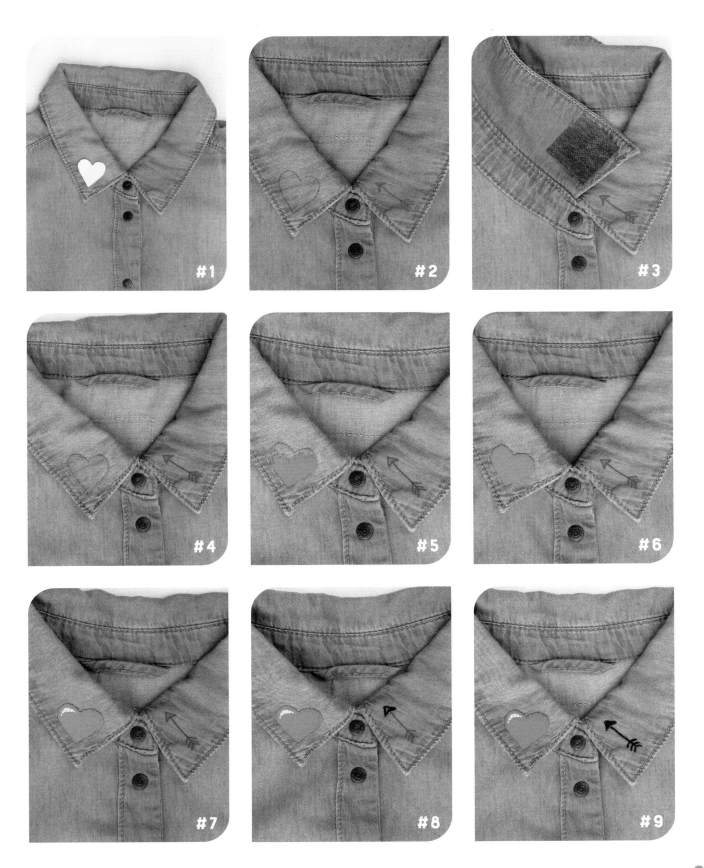

⟫⟫ AZTEC DENIM JACKET

This geometric Aztec design brings a touch of festival-chic to your wardrobe. It will take a little while to complete, due to the scale of it, but you can always downsize it if you prefer.

✖ Find the Aztec template on page 118

YOU WILL NEED
Denim jacket
Tape measure or ruler
Fine-tipped water-soluble fabric pen
Tear-away embroidery stabilizer (optional)
Small embroidery hoop (optional), measuring 4–6in (10–15cm)
Embroidery needle, size 7
Embroidery scissors
Stranded cottons in pastel pink, green, orange, yellow and blue
Thimble

STITCHES
Running stitch (see page 106)
Backstitch (see page 106)
Split stitch (see page 107)
Stem stitch (see page 107)
Chain stitch (see page 108)
Satin stitch (see page 112)
Seed stitch (see page 113)
French knots (see page 115)

NOTE
Use three strands of cotton and a standard 16in (40cm) length throughout.

Tip

For this design, you can choose whether to use a hoop or not. If you do use one, make sure it does not crush any of your embroidery once it is tightened.

STEP 1

Transfer the Aztec template to the back of your jacket using the embroidery transfer paper method (see page 100). Alternatively, to ensure the design fits your jacket exactly, you can measure the width of the back panel on your jacket, then carefully plot out the dimensions of the design using a tape measure or ruler and a water-soluble fabric pen. If you wish, you can alter the design to suit your garment. This design splits the back panel vertically into two sections with a $^3/_8$in- (1cm-) wide bar and is then calculated for five large triangles to run across the top of the bar with six medium-sized triangles fitting in above. Seven smaller triangles run across the bottom, with another eight smaller triangles fitting in between.

Tip

If your jacket is slightly stretchy, then back the reverse of it with reinforcement such as tear-away embroidery stabilizer.

STEP 2

The largest triangles start with three rows of chain stitch in pink. Secure your thread in the bar using the stab-stitch method (see page 104). Make the chain stitches roughly $^1/_8$in (3mm) long and not too tight. Each row starts at the bottom and should sit closely next to each other.

Tip

Where possible, all the threads should be started and finished using the stab-stitch method. If there is no place to finish with a stab stitch, secure the thread on the reverse of the jacket by weaving along the back of the stitches (see page 104).

STEP 3

The next section is worked in five rows of running stitch using green thread. The stitches should be about $^{13}/_{64}$in (5mm) long and placed in a brickwork formation.

STEP 4

The centre of the triangle is worked in scattered French knots using orange thread.

STEP 5

Repeat the same steps for all of the larger triangles.

STEP 6

Now move on to the lower row of triangles. Outline a triangle with a single row of backstitch in yellow; the stitches should be approximately $^5/_{32}$–$^{13}/_{64}$in (4–5mm) long. Next, work zigzags of the same length, again using backstitch.

NOTE: If you wish, you can draw the zigzag lines on with a water-soluble fabric pen.

STEP 7

Using blue thread, work three rows of split stitch, leaving a slight gap between each row.

STEP 8

The centre is worked in green thread using satin stitch. Start in the centre of the triangle with a diagonal stitch.

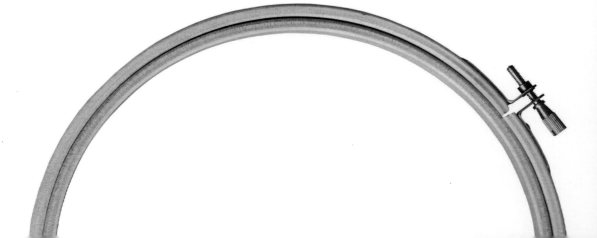

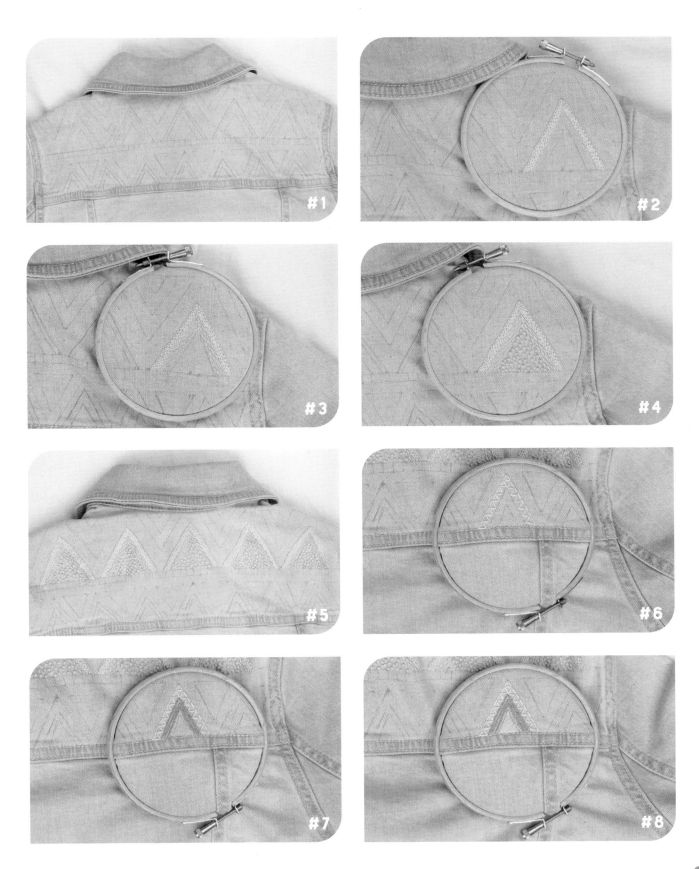

STEP 9

Outline the satin stitch with another row of split stitch in blue. This should sit over the edge of the satin stitch.

STEP 10

Repeat the same steps for all of the lower triangles.

STEP 11

The small triangles in between the lower row and the middle bar are worked alternately in orange and pink. They are filled with seed stitches measuring roughly ⅛–5/32in (3–4mm) and outlined with a single row of stem stitch.

STEP 12

The row running vertically across the centre can be filled with small ⅜in (1cm) squares of satin stitch, using all the colours. You can draw each square on to the jacket to allow for even-sized squares. Bring the needle out on the line ⅜in (1cm) away and take the needle back down where the previous stitches are. This way you will not 'disturb' the other stitches by bringing the needle up in the same hole.

STEP 13

Moving on to the top row of triangles, fill the centre with a small amount of seed stitch using pink thread.

STEP 14

For the next section, use orange thread to work rows of stem stitch. Leave a small gap between each row; you should be able get five to six rows in this area.

STEP 15

Lastly, work the outer edge of the triangle using a single row of split stitch in yellow; the gap can then be filled with a row of split stitch in a zigzag shape. Repeat the same steps for all the triangles.

STEP 16

For the finishing touches, work a single row of French knots evenly between the top and middle set of triangles. Mark the distance out with a pen beforehand. Then, using a thimble if possible, work a row of backstitch in the pink thread along the bottom seam of the panel. This will be very thick – the thimble will help you to push the needle through.

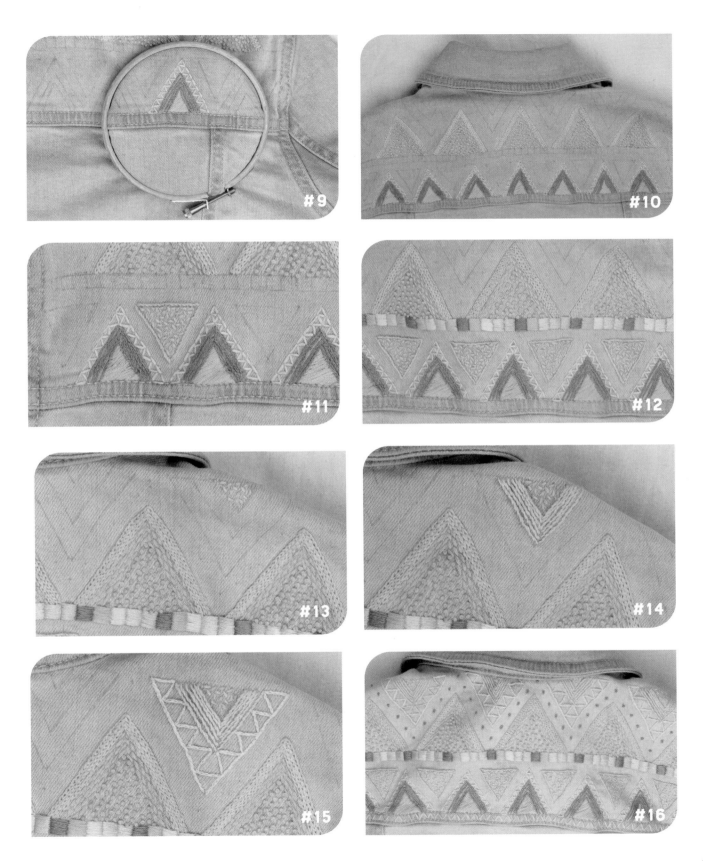

>>> TROPICAL TOTE BAG

Turn a simple tote bag into something more lush with this *Monstera* plant design. It can be worked in your choice of running or backstitch in pastel shades of tapestry wool.

✖ Find the *Monstera* template on page 119

YOU WILL NEED
Paper
Black felt-tipped pen
Cotton tote bag
Fabric pen
Chenille needle, size 24
Embroidery scissors
Tapestry wool in green, grey, pale pink and lilac
Embroidery hoop (optional)
Tapestry needle, size 24
Iron

STITCHES
Running / backstitch (see page 106)
Whipped running / backstitch (see page 107)

NOTE
Use a standard 16in (40cm) length of thread throughout.

STEP 1

Start by tracing the *Monstera* template with a black felt-tipped pen onto a large piece of paper, or two smaller pieces of paper taped together. Make sure you check that it is the right size for your tote bag.

STEP 2

Place the piece of paper inside the bag and trace onto the tote using a fabric pen. If your tote bag is made out of a dark or thick material, transfer the design onto the bag using one of the methods described on pages 99–101.

Tip

As this design is quite large, you may like to use an embroidery hoop. If you do not use one, then take care not to pull your stitches too tightly so as to avoid puckering the fabric.

STEP 3

Thread a length of green tapestry wool through the chenille needle. Starting anywhere on the design line of the bottom left leaf, secure the thread using the stab-stitch method (see page 104). Begin to work a large running stitch or backstitch. Stitches should be approximately $^{13}/_{64}$in (5mm) long. Work along all of the lines. When you have covered the lines of this leaf, secure your thread off along the reverse of your stitches (see page 104).

Tip

You can choose which stitch you would like to work this design in – running stitch or backstitch – as they look the same.

STEP 4

Thread a tapestry needle with a new length of green wool. Secure the thread under the stitches at the top of the leaf using the stab-stitch method. Bring the thread to the front of the bag and 'whip' the stitches by passing the needle and thread carefully under each stitch. Do not pass the needle through the fabric. Make sure you always pass the needle under the stitches from the same side.

STEP 5

Repeat the same process for the top leaf using grey wool.

STEP 6

Now you can work the top left-hand leaf in a plain running or backstitch using pale-pink wool. Make sure you do not stitch over the stitches of the green and grey leaves, but pass the stitches on the reverse.

NOTE: These two leaves are not whipped because they are to appear in the background.

STEP 7

Stitch the remaining leaf in plain running or backstitch using lilac thread. Ensure all the threads on the reverse are secured and there are no loose tails. Finally, carefully press the bag with an iron.

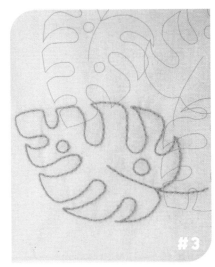

DIFFICULTY LEVEL: 1

PALM-TREE TEE

The perfect summer motif, this palm tree conjures up beach-holiday vibes. It can be worked on any T-shirt using fly stitch and chain stitch.

✖ Find the Palm-tree template on page 120

YOU WILL NEED

Tracing paper or photocopier
T-shirt (with or without a pocket)
Paper
Fabric pen
Embroidery transfer paper or water-soluble transparent plastic (optional)
Tear-away embroidery stabilizer
Embroidery needle, size 7–10
Machine thread in light colour
Embroidery scissors
Stranded cottons in green, dark green and brown
Tweezers or tapestry needle (any size)
Iron

STITCHES

Running stitch (see page 106)
Chain stitch (see page 108)
Fly stitch (see page 114)

NOTE
Use a standard 16in (40cm) length of thread throughout.

STEP 1

Photocopy or trace the Palm-tree template onto a small piece of paper. As this T-shirt is white, the image is easy to see so you can trace it directly on with a fabric pen. If your T-shirt is not a light colour, then try using one of the other transfer methods described on pages 99–101, such as embroidery transfer paper or water-soluble transparent plastic.

STEP 2

To prevent the fabric from puckering or pulling, back the reverse of it with a tear-away embroidery stabilizer. Use a light-coloured machine thread and a large running stitch to tack it into place.

STEP 3

Thread two strands of green stranded cotton through the embroidery needle. Secure the thread at the tip of a leaf using the stab-stitch method (see page 104). The first stitch for each leaf is a single running stitch, roughly $1/8$in (3mm) long. Bring the needle back up and out, parallel to the middle of the running stitch and about $5/64$in (2mm) to the side.

STEP 4

Work a vertical row of fly stitch down each line. You can increase the size of the stitches as you go. Make the secure stitch (stab stitch) roughly the same length as the first single running stitch, and secure the thread off at the bottom of each leaf. Do not be tempted to travel the thread along the reverse because this will pull the fabric.

STEP 5

Continue the same process for all of the leaves. The number of leaves is uneven, so work the next leaf in the same colour and then begin to alternate between dark green and regular green.

STEP 6

Play around with the size of the fly stitch to add depth to the leaves.

STEP 7

When the leaves are complete, take two strands of brown stranded cotton and thread them through the embroidery needle. Starting at the top of the trunk, secure the thread, then work two rows of chain stitch down each line, making sure the stitches are neat, even and measuring roughly $1/8$in (3mm).

STEP 8

To finish, secure the threads on the reverse (see page 104) then remove the tacking threads holding the embroidery stabilizer in place. Tear away any excess embroidery stabilizer (tweezers or a tapestry needle will help remove any little bits) and give the T-shirt a gentle press on the reverse with an iron.

CHERRIES BEACH BAG

Liven up a simple straw beach bag by embroidering this fun and bright design using split stitch, seed stitch and chain stitch in a strong tapestry wool.

✖ Find the Cherries template on page 120

YOU WILL NEED

Wash-away embroidery stabilizer
Water-soluble fabric pen
Pins
Rattan or straw handbag (preferably unlined)
Chenille needle, size 22–24
Tapestry wool (or similar) in red, pink, and green
Thimble (optional)
Embroidery scissors
Water spray

STITCHES

Split stitch (see page 107)
Chain stitch (see page 108)
Seed stitch (see page 113)

NOTE
Use a standard 16in (40cm) length of thread throughout.

Tip

When choosing a bag to work on, remember that you will need to be able to stitch through the main material easily. It will be far simpler if the bag you choose is unlined.

STEP 1

Trace the Cherries template onto a piece of wash-away embroidery stabilizer using a water-soluble fabric pen. Pin the template into place on your bag. (If you prefer, you can tack the design on using machine thread over tissue paper, see page 99.)

STEP 2

Thread a length of red tapestry wool through the chenille needle. Secure the thread on the outline of one of the cherries using the stab-stitch method (see page 104).

STEP 3

Start to work the seed stitch. Your stitches should be approximately $5/32$–$13/64$in (4–5mm) long and worked at random angles to the previous stitch. Try always to work the next stitch towards the previous stitch; this should allow the spacing to stay consistent. Fill the entire cherry with seed stitch, making sure to leave gaps for the 'shiny' patches. Finish the thread by weaving through the stitches on the reverse (see page 104).

STEP 4

Thread a length of pink tapestry wool and secure it on the outline of the cherry using stab stitch. Work a single row of split stitch around the 'shine'. Your stitches should be approximately $1/8$–$5/32$in (3–4mm) long and split in the centre each time. Finish the thread with stab stitch.

STEP 5

Now work a row of split stitch around the outside of the cherry using red tapestry wool. It is best to start at the top of the cherry, so you can finish your thread in the stalk using stab stitch.

STEP 6

Repeat steps 2–5 for the second cherry.

STEP 7

Thread a length of green tapestry wool and secure it at the top of the stalk. Work a row of chain stitch down towards the cherry. Your stitches should be approximately $1/8$–$5/32$in (3–4mm) long and evenly worked. Finish the thread off by weaving along the back of the stitches on the reverse.

STEP 8

Work the second stalk in chain stitch.

STEP 9

To finish, carefully tear away large areas of the stabilizer and remove any small pieces by spraying lightly with water.

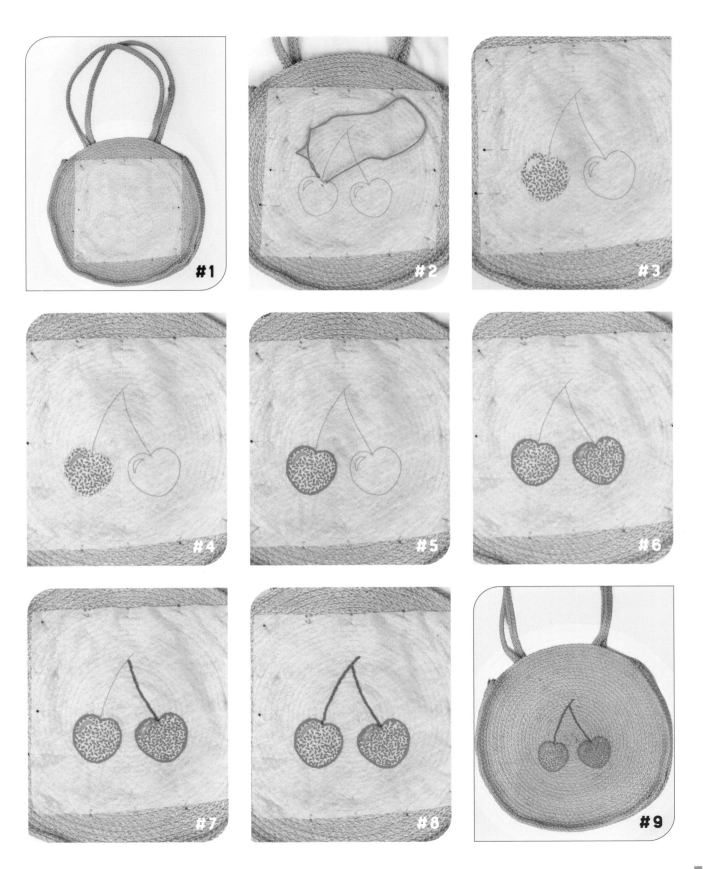

>>> ZODIAC PLANT POTS

Give a mystical edge to your home by embroidering a zodiac symbol onto soft plant pots using thick thread, stem stitch and backstitch.

✖ Find the Zodiac templates on page 121

YOU WILL NEED
Soft rattan pot
Embroidery or fine-tipped scissors
Water-soluble transparent plastic
White gel pen or contrasting-colour permanent pen
Machine thread
Embroidery needle, size 5–7
Chenille needle, size 20–24 (make sure this is large enough for your chosen thread)
Crochet thread (or similar thick thread) in turquoise, blue and green tones
Tapestry wool (for embroidering large designs) in turquoise, blue and green tones

STITCHES
Running stitch (see page 106)
Backstitch (see page 106)
Stem stitch (see page 107)

> **NOTE**
> Use a standard 16in (40cm) length of thread throughout.

STEP 1

Take a soft rattan pot. If it is designed to hold plants, it will most likely have a plastic lining. This should be carefully unpicked, snipping the stitches with embroidery scissors along the side you want to work on.

NOTE: You do not need to unpick the entire lining; you just need enough room to get your hand in between it and the pot.

STEP 2

Cut out a piece of water-soluble transparent plastic that is slightly larger than your chosen zodiac sign. Trace the zodiac sign onto the plastic using a white gel pen or a permanent pen in a contrasting colour.

STEP 3

Decide whereabouts on the pot you want to position the zodiac sign. Then, place the plastic directly on the pot and tack it into place using machine thread and a large running stitch.

STEP 4

Thread a length of turquoise crochet thread (or a similar thick thread) through the chenille needle. Secure the thread along the bottom line of the design using the stab-stitch method (see page 104) and work a row of stem stitch. Make sure your stitches are quite long – approximately $5/32 - 13/64$in (4–5mm).

Tip

The rattan is a coarse material to work through, so keep checking the condition of your thread.

STEP 5

Repeat along the top row, being mindful to keep the stitches slightly shorter when going around a curve so as to create a smooth appearance. Secure the threads off along the reverse of the stitches (see page 104).

STEP 6

Now change over to a different tone of thread. Work a row of backstitch directly underneath the stem stitch. Your stitches should be quite long – approximately $5/32 - 13/64$in (4–5mm).

STEP 7

Remove the tacking stitches and tear away the plastic. If any plastic remains, gently spray it with water and it will quickly disappear.

STEP 8

The same steps can be repeated for the other zodiac signs, using slightly different tones of thread.

STEP 9

For bigger pots, simply increase the size of the zodiac sign and use a nice chunky thread, such as a tapestry wool.

#1

#2

#3

#4

#5

#6

#7

#8

#9

≫ ASTRO CAP

Tap into the cosmic trend by stitching our solar system onto a baseball cap using stranded cottons and metallic threads.

✖ Find the Astro template on page 121

YOU WILL NEED
Plain navy-blue baseball cap
Circle template
White embroidery pencil
Ruler
Embroidery needle, size 7–10
Embroidery scissors
Stranded cottons in red, yellow, cream, lilac, turquoise, blue, pale blue, orange, white and green
Metallic embroidery threads in grey and variegated

STITCHES
Backstitch (see page 106)
Cross stitch (see page 110)
Seed stitch (see page 113)

Tip

Take care when working with metallic threads, as they can break easily. If possible, use a needle with a large eye.

NOTE
Use a standard 16in (40cm) length of thread throughout.

STEP 1

Take a plain navy-blue baseball cap and draw on the planets using a circle template and a white embroidery pencil. Use the Astro template on page 121 as a guide. You can choose the layout of the planets, and do not worry about marking out the stars. Make sure to include the two comets, using a ruler to achieve nice straight edges.

Tip

Place something flat and firm inside the cap when drawing onto it.

STEP 2

Beginning with the planet Mars, thread two strands of red stranded cotton through the embroidery needle. Secure the thread using the stab-stitch method (see page 104) and stitch a neat, even row of backstitch around the circle, working inwards to create a small spiral. The stitches should be approximately 1/8in (3mm) long. Finish the thread on the reverse of the cap by weaving along the back of the stitches (see page 104).

STEP 3

Using two strands of yellow stranded cotton, fill in the gaps between the red spiral with backstitch.

STEP 4

For the planet Mercury, work an outline in backstitch, using two strands of cream stranded cotton; work curved vertical lines, leaving a gap between each row. Then, using two strands of variegated metallic thread, fill in the gaps on one side of the planet, working the rows in a variety of lengths to create a curved illusion.

STEP 5

Repeat the same steps for the planets Venus, Jupiter and Neptune. For Venus, use the red stranded cotton for the main stitches and the variegated metallic threads for the shading. For Jupiter, use the cream stranded cotton for the main colour and the variegated metallic threads for the shading. For Neptune, use the turquoise stranded cotton for the main colour and pale blue for the shading.

STEP 6

Saturn and Uranus should be the primary features of the cap. It is best to stitch the rings around them first by working two rows of backstitch in the metallic thread. They can then be worked in the same way as the previous planets. Saturn's main area is worked using lilac and cream for the shading, and the ring is worked in gold variegated metallic threads. Uranus's main area is worked using pale green and turquoise for the shading and the ring is worked in grey metallic threads.

STEP 7

Planet Earth can be worked slightly differently. First outline it with two strands of blue stranded cotton, then work a random backstitch to create the illusion of the sea. Fill the remaining space with green stranded cotton and stitch several vertical rows on top of the green and blue in white stranded cotton to create clouds.

STEP 8

For the two comets, start by working the top section with a backstitch in white stranded cotton, then move to the yellow for the mid-section, before working the tails with orange stranded cotton.

STEP 9

For the stars you can be as varied as you like. For the tiny dots just work a small, but open, seed stitch. The mid-sized stars can be worked in a simple cross stitch and the larger stars can be worked in a larger cross stitch with one or two more stitches on top. Finish all the threads off along the reverse of the cap by weaving them along the back of the stitches.

Tip

Be mindful not to travel long threads along the reverse of the cap when working the stars; not only can they get caught and damaged, they can also give the cap a puckered appearance.

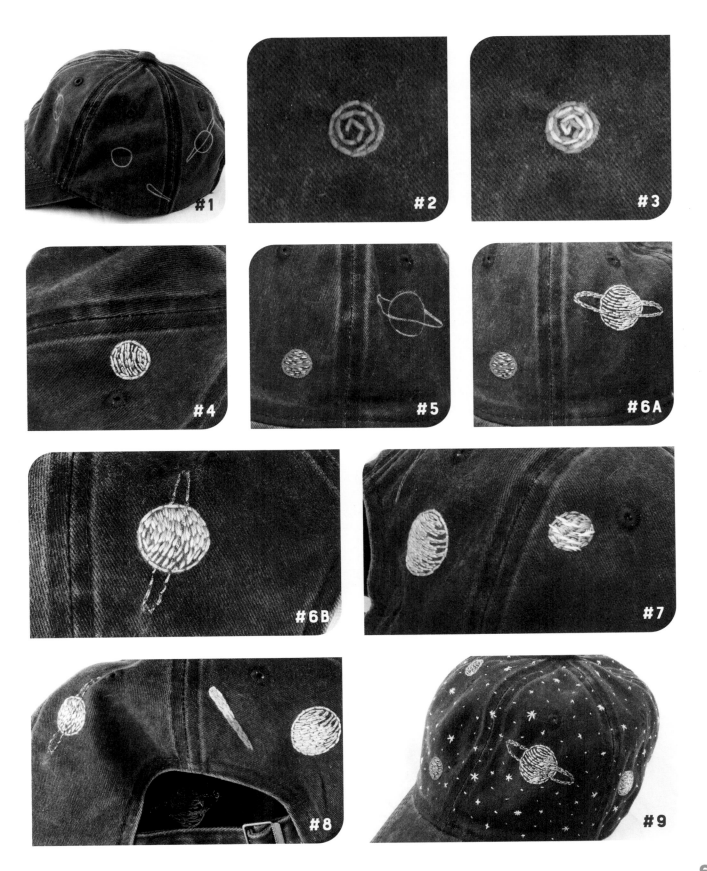

#1

#2

#3

#4

#5

#6A

#6B

#7

#8

#9

PINEAPPLE NOTEBOOK

Make a plain and simple notebook stand out from the crowd by embroidering this fun, vibrant pineapple design directly onto the cover in trellis stitch.

✳ Find the Pineapple template on page 122

YOU WILL NEED
Notebook with thin card cover
Sharp pencil
Tracing paper (optional)
Tapestry needle, size 24
Embroidery scissors
Thick embroidery threads, e.g. stranded cotton or Perle, in light green, dark green, yellow and orange
Chenille needle, size 24
Ruler
Paper, similar colour to notebook cover (optional)
Glue stick (optional)

STITCHES
Running stitch (see page 106)
Double running stitch (see page 106)
Trellis stitch (see page 111)

NOTE
Use a standard 16in (40cm) length of thread throughout.

Tip

Avoid using a notebook with a thick card cover, as it will be difficult to stitch through.

STEP 1

Take your notebook and use a sharp pencil to draw by eye the outline of the pineapple onto the cover. If you don't feel confident doing this, you can trace the template onto tracing paper using a heavy-leaded pencil. Turn the tracing paper over and place it onto the notebook. Trace over the reverse of the tracing to transfer the design.

STEP 2

Start with the small dark-green leaves. Thread the tapestry needle with a length of dark-green thread. You will need to pierce a hole through the card before each stitch using a sharp chenille needle. Start your thread with a knot at the top, a few stitches away from where you will begin stitching. Make sure you catch down the thread on the reverse of the work by piercing the thread with your stitching (and check you are doing this throughout by turning the cover over regularly to see).

STEP 3

Start to work a row of running stitch along the pencil lines. Be sure to keep your stitches and gaps the same length. Cut off the waste knot before you reach it, making sure it is secure at the back.

STEP 4

When you reach the end, go back in the opposite direction, filling in the gaps left between each stitch. This creates a double running stitch. Once you have reached the end of the thread you can secure it by weaving through the reverse of the stitches (see page 104).

STEP 5

Repeat this process for all of the small dark-green leaves.

STEP 6

Now work the large dark-green leaves in the same way. To save time here, you can pierce all the holes first, then work along in running stitch before coming back and making it a double running stitch.

STEP 7

Now work the remaining leaves using the light-green thread in the same double running stitch. Once you have reached the end of the thread you can secure it by weaving through the reverse of the stitches.

STEP 8

When you have completed all of the leaves you can start to work the main body of the pineapple in trellis stitch. Thread the tapestry needle with a length of orange thread. Remember to pierce the card with the chenille needle first; then start your thread on the right-hand side of the pineapple and angle it approximately 45 degrees down to the left-hand side. Bring the needle back up again on the left-hand side, approximately $^{13}/_{64}$in (5mm) above the previous stitch.

STEP 9

Continue working the stitch up to the top of the pineapple, being careful to keep the distance between each stitch at $^{13}/_{64}$in (5mm). Use a ruler to help. When the top half is worked, weave the thread along the reverse of the stitches to avoid long trailing threads, then work the bottom half of the pineapple.

STEP 10

Thread a new length of orange thread and work the stitches laying in the opposite direction over the first set of stitches. Keep the distance between each stitch the same and the angle at approximately 45 degrees.

STEP 11

Trellis stitch needs to be caught down with small securing stitches to prevent it from moving around. Pierce the card first with the chenille needle, then secure the yellow thread on the side of the pineapple and work in diagonal rows from the centre of each diamond to just over the top. The stitches should be worked in the same order for each row, i.e. top to bottom, and only need to be approximately $^{5}/_{64}$–$^{1}/_{8}$in (2–3mm) long.

STEP 12

When all the securing stitches are complete, thread the tapestry needle with a length of orange thread and work a row of double running stitch around the entire body of the pineapple. You should not need to pierce any holes for this, as the trellis stitch is worked in the same area. When you have finished stitching, press any obvious holes in the card closed with the tip of the tapestry needle. If you prefer to hide all the reverse stitches, carefully glue a similar colour piece of paper over the inside front cover. Avoid using glue that is runny – a glue stick is best for this.

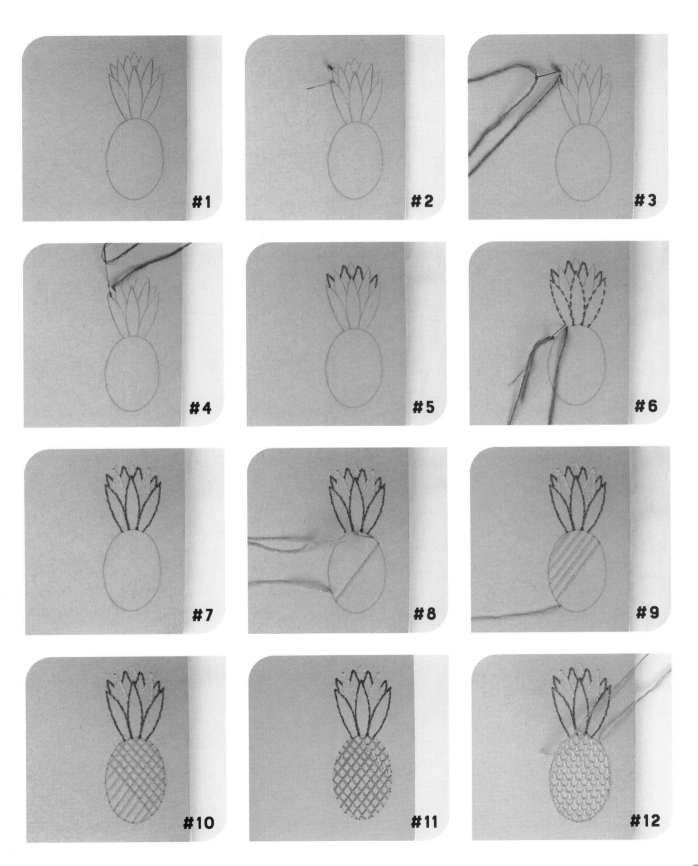

⫸ LIPS MAKE-UP BAG

Add some fun and glamour to a simple make-up bag by embroidering on bright-red lips worked in French knots, stem stitch and satin stitch.

✖ Find the Lips template on page 122

YOU WILL NEED
Tissue paper
Blue coloured pencil
Make-up bag
Pins
Embroidery needle, size 7–10
Embroidery scissors
Machine cotton in pale blue
Tapestry needle or tweezers
Stranded cotton in black, red, pale pink
   and white

STITCHES
Running stitch (see page 106)
Stem stitch (see page 107)
Satin stitch (see page 112)
French knots (see page 115)

NOTE
Use a standard 16in (40cm) length of thread throughout.

STEP 1

Trace the Lips template onto a piece of tissue paper using a blue pencil (blue is a colour that will not show up if it is accidentally transferred onto the fabric).

STEP 2

Position the tracing paper centrally on your make-up bag and pin it into place. Make sure your pins are clean.

STEP 3

Thread the embroidery needle with a length of pale-blue machine cotton. Starting in the middle of the design, make a large running stitch. Do not secure the thread too tightly, as it will be removed at the end of the project; simply go over the first stitch three times. Work the running stitch using a long stitch on the top and a short thread underneath. The stitches should be approximately $^{13}/_{64}$–$^{3}/_{8}$in (5–10mm) long.

STEP 4

When you have covered all of the blue pencil lines with running stitch, carefully rip away the tissue paper. Use tweezers or a tapestry needle to remove any small pieces that remain. You will be left with the outline of the lips.

STEP 5

Now thread three strands of black stranded cotton through the embroidery needle. Starting in the centre of the mouth, work a small and even row of satin stitch.

NOTE: You can start and finish all the threads anywhere within the design using the stab-stitch method (see page 104), as they will all be covered.

STEP 6

Using three strands of black stranded cotton, work a row of stem stitch along the outer and inner edge of the bottom lip, going over the bottom of the black satin stitch. Make your stitches approximately $^{1}/_{8}$in (3mm) long. You can remove the blue tacking stitches as you complete each area.

Tip

If there is no space to secure off your finished threads with a stab stitch, you can secure them instead by weaving the needle through the reverse of the stitches (see page 104).

STEP 7

Starting in the bottom centre of the lower lip, begin to work tightly packed French knots using three strands of red stranded cotton. Leave a space for the 'highlights', then work these areas in pale pink. Make sure none of the fabric can be seen between the knots. The stem stitch should act like a wall holding the French knots within it.

STEP 8

You can now work the two teeth in vertical rows of satin stitch, using three strands of white stranded cotton. When the two teeth are complete, outline them in stem stitch using three strands of black stranded cotton.

STEP 9

You are now ready to work the top lip. Start by outlining the entire lip in stem stitch, using three strands of black stranded cotton. Then, as before, fill the lip completely with French knots, using three strands of red stranded cotton and three strands of pale-pink stranded cotton for the highlights. When you are happy that the design is complete, carefully remove the pale-blue tacking thread.

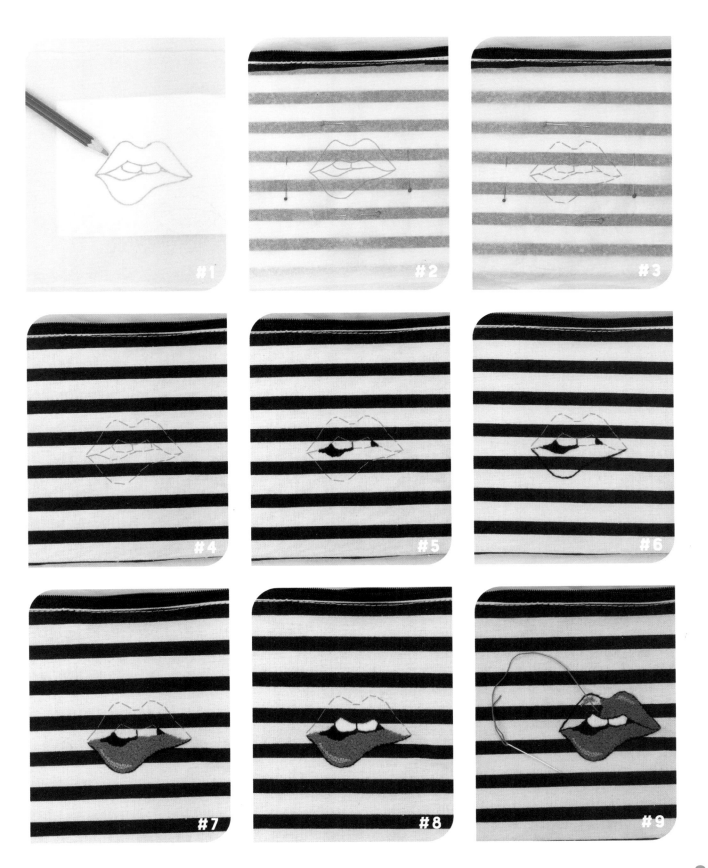

>>> STRAW SUN HAT

Get your sun hat beach ready! This simple project uses classic running stitch and thick yarn.

✖ Find the Sun and Waves template on page 122

YOU WILL NEED

Water-soluble fabric pen
Wash-away embroidery stabilizer
Craft scissors
Wide-brimmed straw sun hat
Pins
Chenille needle, size 22–24
Embroidery scissors
Thick black yarn, e.g. tapestry or knitting wool
    (I have used a knitting wool with a touch of silver)
Tweezers or water spray

STITCHES

Running stitch (see page 106)
Double running stitch (see page 106)

NOTE
Use a standard 16in (40cm) length of thread throughout.

STEP 1

Using a water-soluble fabric pen, trace the Sun and Waves template onto a piece of wash-away embroidery stabilizer and cut it into the shape of the brim of the hat. Decide where you would like the design to sit on the brim, then pin it into position.

STEP 2

Thread the chenille needle with a length of thick black yarn. Secure the yarn on the design line at the end of the wave using the stab-stitch method (see page 104).

STEP 3

Work a single row of running stitch along the wave. Your stitches should be approximately $5/32-13/64$in (4–5mm) long with a gap in between of the same length.

Tip

Make sure you keep all of the stitches and gaps the same distance throughout the design, and the back of the stitches just as neat as the front.

STEP 4

When you reach the end of the line, work back towards the start of the wave, filling in the gaps. This is now a double running stitch. You should not be piercing the stitches but sharing the holes. Once you reach the end of the wave, secure the thread along the back by weaving through the stitches (see page 104).

STEP 5

Now you can work the sun. Starting with your yarn on the circle, stitch each ray of the sun followed by a running stitch on the circle. Work in this way all around the sun.

STEP 6

When you have returned to the beginning stitch, fill in the gaps on the sun with a double running stitch. Take care with the stitches on the reverse. Make sure it still looks like a sun.

STEP 7

Repeat steps 3–4 for the second wave.

STEP 8

Once the stitching is complete, carefully remove the stabilizer by tearing it away. If any small pieces remain, you can either remove them with tweezers or lightly spray them with water and they will disappear.

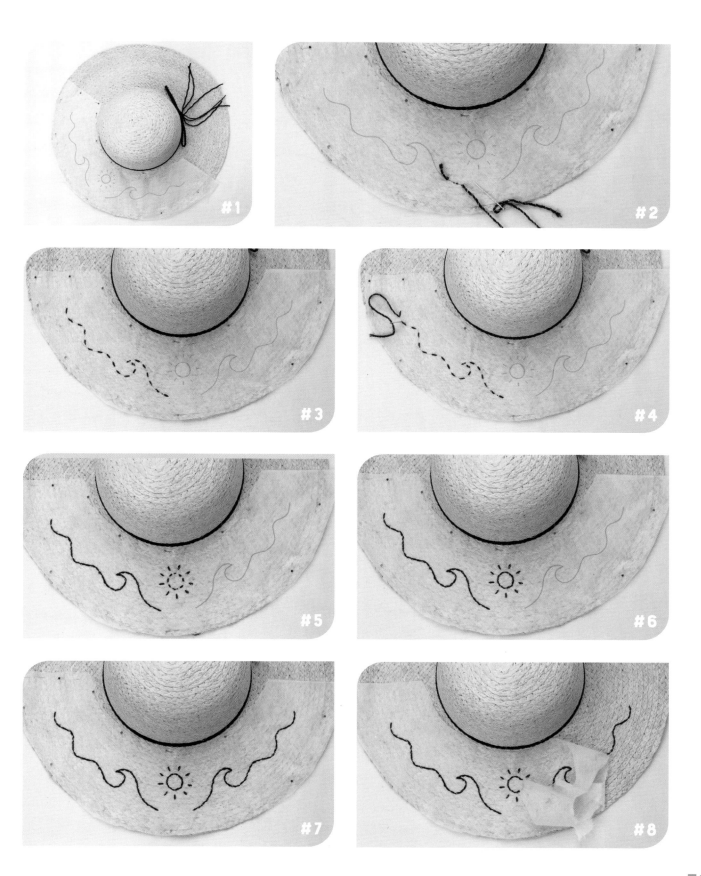

>>> SNAKE BLOUSE

Inspired by the snakes adorning collections from famous fashion houses, this simple but quirky snake adds interest to a plain blouse or shirt. It uses satin, stem and running stitch.

✖ Find the Snake template on page 123

YOU WILL NEED
Buttoned blouse or shirt
Water-soluble fabric pen
Tear-away embroidery stabilizer
   (optional, depending on blouse material)
Pins (optional)
Machine thread (optional)
Embroidery needle, size 10
Embroidery scissors
Stranded cottons in orange, black and yellow
Cotton bud
Iron

STITCHES
Running stitch (see page 106)
Stem stitch (see page 107)
Satin stitch (see page 112)

NOTE
Use a standard 16in (40cm) length of thread throughout.

STEP 1

Take a blouse or a shirt with a button-down front and draw on a snake using a water-soluble fabric pen. You can use the template provided on page 123 or draw it on by freehand so that it works for your particular garment; for instance, you may want it to be longer or for it to have more curves.

STEP 2

If the fabric of your blouse is very delicate or has a slight stretch, use tear-away embroidery stabilizer on the reverse. Start by pinning it into place then tack it using machine cotton and a large running stitch.

STEP 3

Thread the embroidery needle with a single strand of orange stranded cotton. Starting in the centre of the snake's head, secure the thread using the stab-stitch method (see page 104). Begin to work vertical satin stitches from the centre of the head towards the top.

NOTE: With satin stitch you normally need to first work a row of split stitch on the outlines; for this design, it will not be necessary as the snake is outlined in black stem stitch.

STEP 4

When you have worked the top section of the snake's head, go back to the centre and continue to work the satin stitch down the body of the snake. Make sure your stitches stay vertical and that no gaps show between them. Work the last stitches over the seam line to create the illusion that the snake is in between the layers.

STEP 5

Next work the lower jaw of the head in satin stitch. Using a single strand of yellow stranded cotton, start in the centre of the shape. It is best to take the needle out on the lower edge of the jaw and down where the orange stitches meet. This means you will not disturb the first set of stitches.

STEP 6

Using a single strand of black stranded cotton, work a neat row of stem stitch around the outline and to form the forked tongue. Make sure you follow the direction rule for stem stitch (see page 107).

STEP 7

Continue the rest of the body, working with satin stitch in vertical stripes of orange and yellow. Be mindful of your tension and try to work the stitches right up to the outer edge.

STEP 8

Outline the outer edges with stem stitch in black stranded cotton and in between each section of orange and yellow.

STEP 9

Repeat the same steps for the next section of the body and the tail. When you have completed all of the sections, carefully remove the tacking threads (if using embroidery reinforcement) and tear or cut away any of the excess. Remove any pen marks using a wet cotton bud and gently press the reverse of the blouse with a cool iron.

Tip

Make sure to bring the needle out and in close to the previous stitches, and to not pull them too tight, otherwise the fabric will pucker.

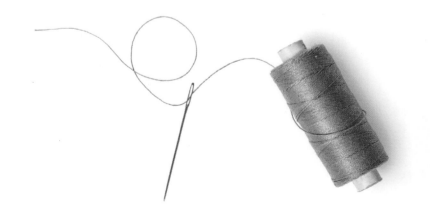

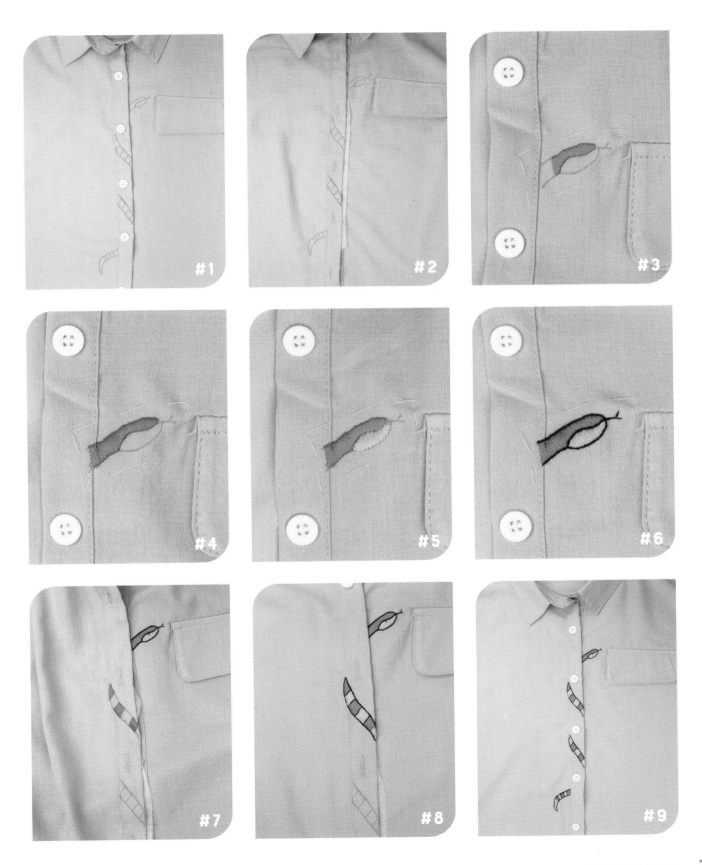

>>> AVOCADO SOCKS

Add a little pop of colour to a pair of plain socks with this cute avocado motif worked in split stitch.

✖ Find the Avocado template on page 123

YOU WILL NEED
Cotton socks
Water-soluble plastic (optional, depending on type of socks)
Fine-tipped fabric pen (waterproof, optional)
Embroidery stabilizer
Embroidery needle, size 7–10
Machine thread in light colour
Stranded cottons in light brown, avocado green, dark brown and dark green
Embroidery scissors

STITCHES
Running stitch (see page 106)
Split stitch (see page 107)

> **NOTE**
> Use a standard 16in (40cm) length of thread throughout.

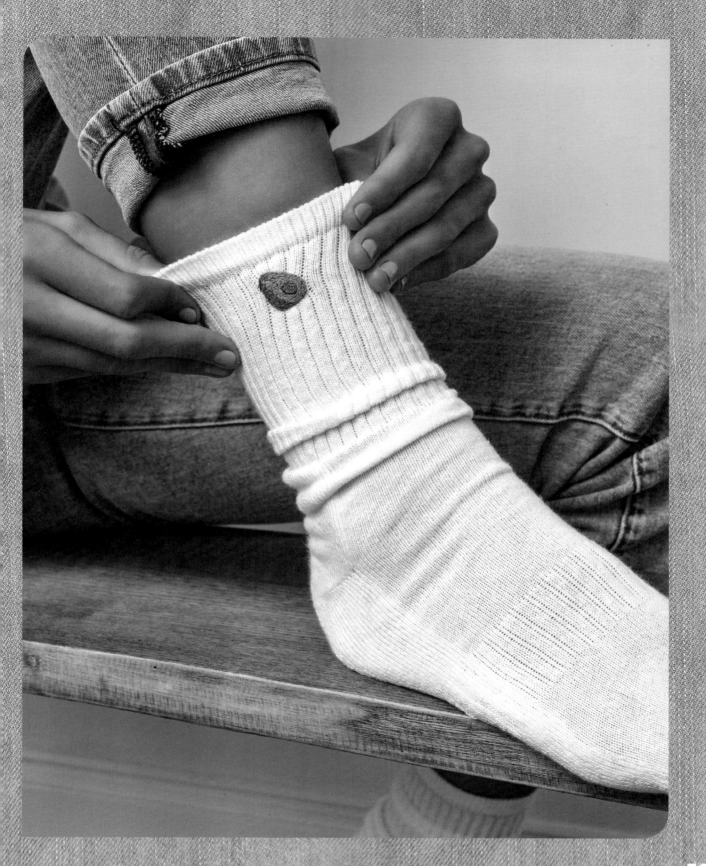

STEP 1

The socks that have been used here are plain sports socks with a slight stretch. Because of the ribbing and stretch, it is best to trace the Avocado template onto water-soluble plastic using a fine-tipped waterproof pen in a contrasting colour to the socks. However, if you are using socks with no ribbing, you can trace the design directly on using a fine-tipped fabric pen. Decide where you would like the avocado to sit.

STEP 2

It is essential to back the inside of the socks with embroidery stabilizer to prevent the embroidery from pulling once the socks are worn. Tack the plastic and the stabilizer into place at the same time, using a large running stitch in a light-coloured machine thread.

STEP 3

Thread the embroidery needle with two strands of light-brown stranded cotton and secure with stab stitches (see page 104) on the stone area of the avocado. Work a neat and even split stitch, starting from the outside of the stone. Make sure the stitches are small – approximately $^3/_{64}$–$^5/_{64}$in (1–2mm) long.

STEP 4

Continue to work the split stitch inwards, making sure there are no gaps in between each row. Secure the thread off along the reverse by weaving through the stitches (see page 104).

STEP 5

Now thread two strands of avocado-green stranded cotton and work another set of split stitch, starting from the design line and working inwards. Leave a small gap at the base of the stone for a shadow.

STEP 6

Work a single row of split stitch along the bottom edge of the stone using two strands of the dark-brown stranded cotton.

STEP 7

Lastly work the skin of the avocado in two strands of the dark-green stranded cotton, starting on the outside and keeping your stitches neat and even.

STEP 8

Remove the tacking thread and pull away the plastic. You can also dip the socks in water – the plastic will quickly disappear.

STEP 9

Repeat the steps again on the other sock, remembering to reverse the design.

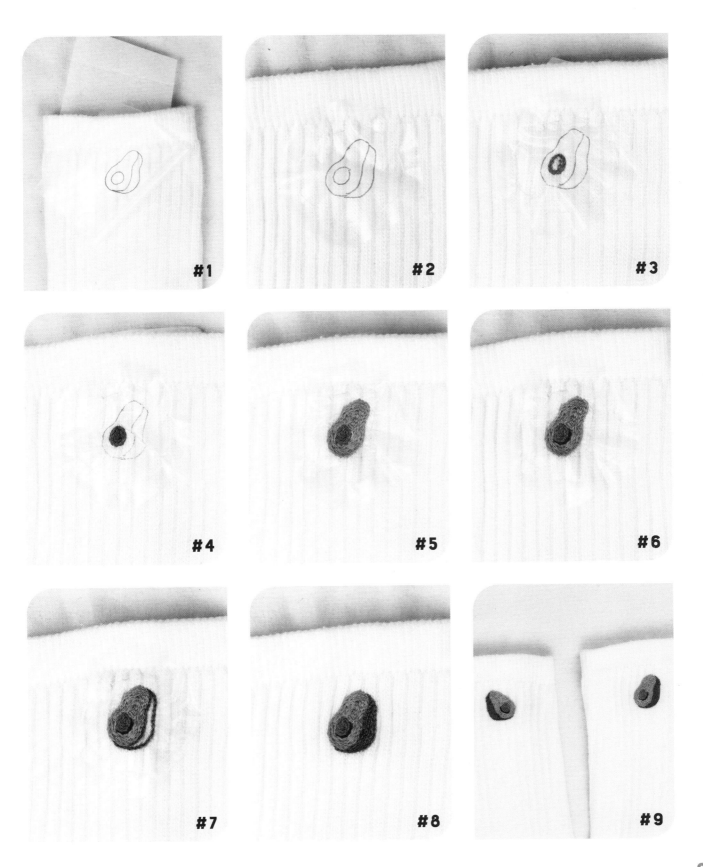

⋙ SWALLOWS JACKET

Add classic tattoo-style swallows to the sleeve and pocket of a jacket using chain stitch and backstitch in stranded cottons.

✖ Find the Swallows template on page 123

YOU WILL NEED
A photocopier or tracing paper
Paper
Craft scissors
Jacket
Embroidery transfer paper
Ballpoint pen
Fabric pen
Tear-away embroidery stabilizer (optional)
Embroidery needle, size 7–10
Embroidery scissors
Stranded cottons in yellow, blue, dark grey and red

STITCHES
Backstitch (see page 106)
Chain stitch (see page 108)

> **NOTE**
> Use a standard 16in (40cm) length of thread throughout.

STEP 1

Photocopy or trace each swallow onto a piece of paper. Take your jacket and place one swallow on a sleeve and the other on a pocket (see Tip below). Position the embroidery transfer paper underneath the swallows and draw over them with a ballpoint pen, pressing firmly down. When the papers are removed, draw over the designs using a fabric pen.

NOTE: If your jacket is slightly stretchy, back the reverse of the jacket with tear-away embroidery stabilizer.

Tip

Make sure you can get your hand comfortably inside the sleeve and pocket before transferring the design, as embroidering can be tricky if they are tight.

STEP 2

Thread the embroidery needle with two strands of yellow stranded cotton. Starting with the back wing, secure the thread at the top of the wing using the stab-stitch method (see page 104). Work a small and neat row of chain stitch, approximately $5/64$–$1/8$in (2–3mm) long. Take care to catch just the pocket and not the main fabric of the jacket.

Tip

Where possible, all threads should be started and finished with the stab-stitch method. If there is no place to finish with a stab stitch, secure the thread on the reverse of the jacket by weaving along the back of the stitches (see page 104).

STEP 3

Thread two strands of blue stranded cotton and work vertical, downward rows of chain stitch to create the wing feathers.

STEP 4

Outline the outer edges of the wing and feathers with a small, $5/64$–$1/8$in (2–3mm), single row of backstitch using two strands of dark-grey stranded cotton.

STEP 5

Continue to fill the body with blue chain stitch, starting from the outside and working inwards.

STEP 6

Fill the belly with two rows of chain stitch, using two strands of red stranded cotton. When this is done, outline all the areas with backstitch, using two strands of dark-grey stranded cotton.

STEP 7

Now work the front wing in the same way as the back wing.

STEP 8

Work the head in the same way as the body, starting the chain stitch from the outside and working inwards. Outline with backstitch in dark grey, as before. Once the stitching is complete, you can cut or tear away the stabilizer if you used it.

STEP 9

Repeat the exact same process for the swallow on the sleeve.

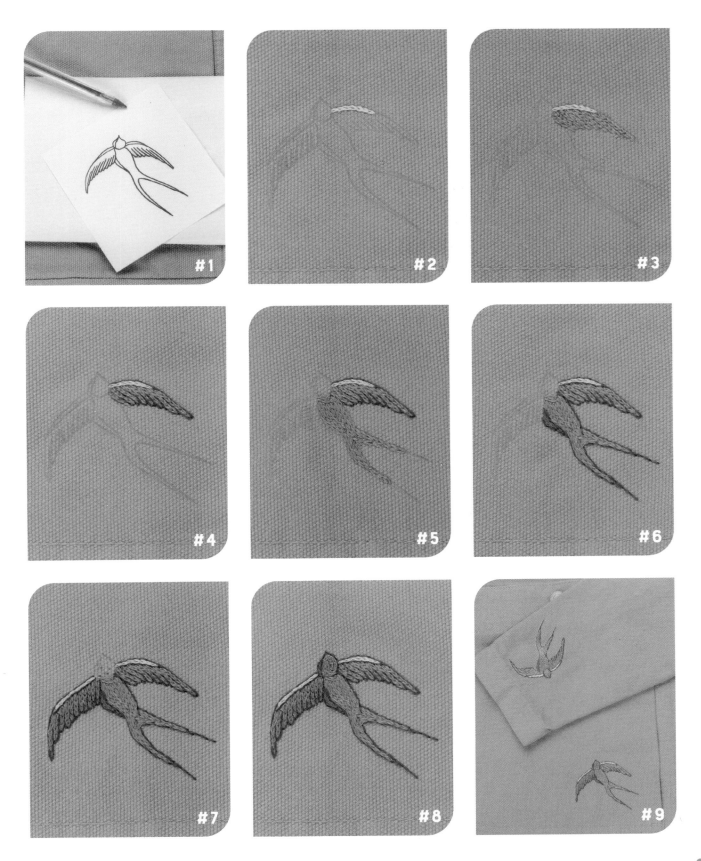

FRENCH-BULLDOG HOOP

This cheeky French bulldog will liven up a plain wall. It is mainly worked in long-and-short stitch, with the addition of laid stitch and split stitch. Details such as the nose are worked in padded satin stitch and French knots.

✖ Find the French-bulldog template on page 123

Tip

As this project uses multiple colours of thread at the same time, you will need several embroidery needles to hand.

NOTE
Use a standard 16in (40cm) length of thread throughout.

YOU WILL NEED
Closely woven non-stretch fabric, e.g. cotton or linen
Fabric scissors
Iron
Tracing paper or photocopier
Plain paper
Lightbox or window
Sticky tape (optional)
Fine-tipped water-soluble fabric pen
Embroidery hoop, 6–8in (15–20cm)
Embroidery needles, size 10
Chenille needle, size 24
Embroidery scissors
Stranded cotton in pale pink, tan, dark pink, white, mid blue, black and pale blue
Metallic embroidery thread in silver

STITCHES
Split stitch (see page 107)
Padded satin stitch (see page 112)
Laid stitch (see page 113)
Long-and-short (see page 114)
French knots (see page 115)

STEP 1

Cut the fabric to the correct size. When using a hoop frame, it is best to have excess fabric so that the fabric can remain tight. Iron the fabric and prepare the template of the bulldog by photocopying or tracing it onto a piece of paper.

STEP 2

Place the template centrally onto the fabric, then carefully trace the bulldog using a fine-tipped water-soluble fabric pen. If you have a lightbox you can use this to help you. If you do not have a lightbox you can tape the paper to a well-lit window.

STEP 3

Place the fabric into the embroidery hoop, making sure the fabric is as tight as a drum. It is important that the fabric is kept tight throughout the stitching; otherwise, when you come to remove the fabric from the hoop, you are likely to have ripples in it.

STEP 4

When working a design in long-and-short stitch you must first outline the outer edges of each section with a tiny row of split stitch in a matching colour to the long-and-short. The smaller the stitch, the stronger it will be. It will create an inner wall for your long-and-short stitches to go over. Using a size 10 needle and two strands of pale-pink stranded cotton, make a secure stab stitch (see page 104) on the design line, or just inside. Work a single line of split stitch that is approximately $5/64$in (2mm) long on the outer edge of one ear.

STEP 5

Finish off the old thread using stab stitch and start up a new length of two strands of pale pink. Starting in the middle of the ear, $3/8$in (1cm) below the tip, begin to work the long-and-short stitches to the right-hand side of the ear, taking the stitches down onto the design line. Your stitches should be random lengths, approximately $9/32$–$3/8$in (7–10mm) long. Take care not to overlap or twist threads and to ensure that no fabric is showing.

Tip

Always work the shapes from the centre outwards. This will ensure the angle of your stitches remain the same.

STEP 6

Go back to the centre and take the stitches over the split stitch. Make sure you angle the needle inwards so that the stitch 'hugs' the split stitch. No split stitch should be visible.

STEP 7

Now drop down and go back to the centre of the ear. Split the stitches above from behind, bringing the needle down into the fabric. Make sure the stitches come out at random places to create a smooth appearance. Keep working from the centre out to keep the angle true. When you reach the split-stitch edge you must always take the stitch up and over the split stitch.

STEP 8

Work this technique all the way to the base of the ear, making sure you see none of the fabric.

STEP 9

Thread two strands of tan stranded cotton through the embroidery needle. Starting at the base, work another small and tight split stitch over the tip of the ear. Make sure this sits just on top of the edge of the pink long-and-short stitches.

STEP 10

Starting with two new strands of tan stranded cotton, work a satin stitch over the split stitch. Work the top half first, taking the needle out on the left edge and down on the right. When you have reached the top, go back down and work the bottom.

STEP 11

Work the right-hand ear, repeating steps 4–10, taking care to mirror the satin stitch in the other direction. You can add some darker pink to the long-and-short stitches to break up the pale pink by stroking in random stitches among the bottom row.

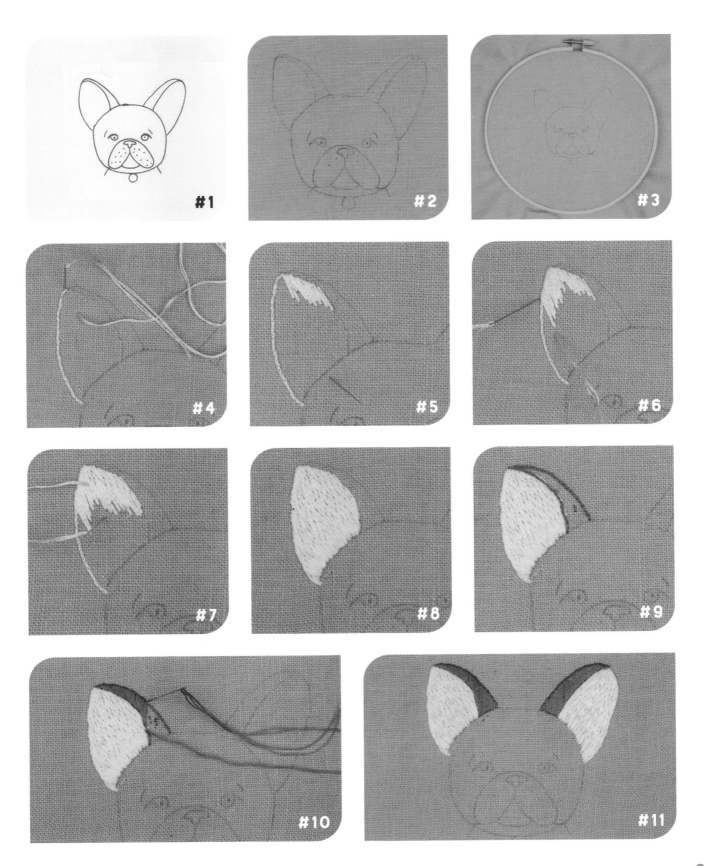

STEP 12

Stitch a single line of long-and-short stitches in two strands of white stranded cotton for the neck.

STEP 13

Split stitch in two strands of the mid-blue stranded cotton on the lower half of the collar. When this is complete, thread a new needle and work a straight set of satin stitch down over the split stitch.

STEP 14

Using two strands of white stranded cotton, split stitch on the lower edge of the chin. This time you will take your first stitch down over the split stitch, then split these stitches from behind, but working in an upwards direction.

STEP 15

Decide where you would like your bulldog to have patches, then draw them on. You now need to work the entire head in long-and-short stitch, starting with a row of split stitch around the main edge, changing from white to tan, where necessary, for the tan patches. Start your long-and-short stitches in the centre top of the head, working the first set of stitches up and over the top split stitch. (Remember to keep your stitches roughly the same length even when near the sides.) When you drop down, your stitches will reverse and you should split the previous stitches from the reverse and work the stitches downwards. Take care to change colour when required for the patches.

NOTE: Do not stitch over the eyes or nose.

STEP 16

Work a single row of split stitch for the outline in two strands of tan stranded cotton. Now pad the bulldog's muzzle in two layers. Use the chenille needle and six strands of tan stranded cotton. Work the first row of padding narrowly in laid stitch, then work another row over this in the opposite direction.

STEP 17

Work satin stitch in two strands of tan stranded cotton over the padding and split stitch. Repeat for both sides of the muzzle, leaving a gap for the nose. Always make sure your last row of padding lays in the opposite direction to your top satin stitch.

STEP 18

Work random French knots in two strands of black stranded cotton over the muzzle. Take care not to disturb the padded satin.

STEP 19

Fill the nose with clusters of French knots, using two strands of pink stranded cotton. Work the eyes in French knots, with black stranded cotton for the pupils and pale-blue stranded cotton for the rest.

STEP 20

Using two strands of black stranded cotton, work a single row of split stitch for the upper eyes and eyebrows.

STEP 21

Lastly, work the dog tag in split stitch and satin stitch using two strands of silver metallic embroidery thread. Start by working a single row of split stitch on the design line, then cover the split stitch with satin stitch, working from the centre out.

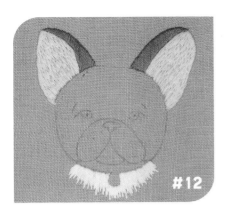

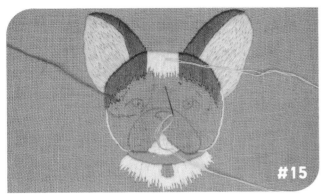

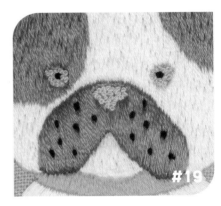

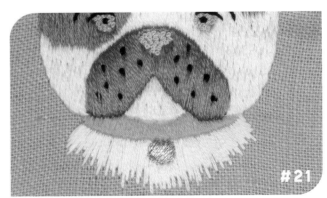

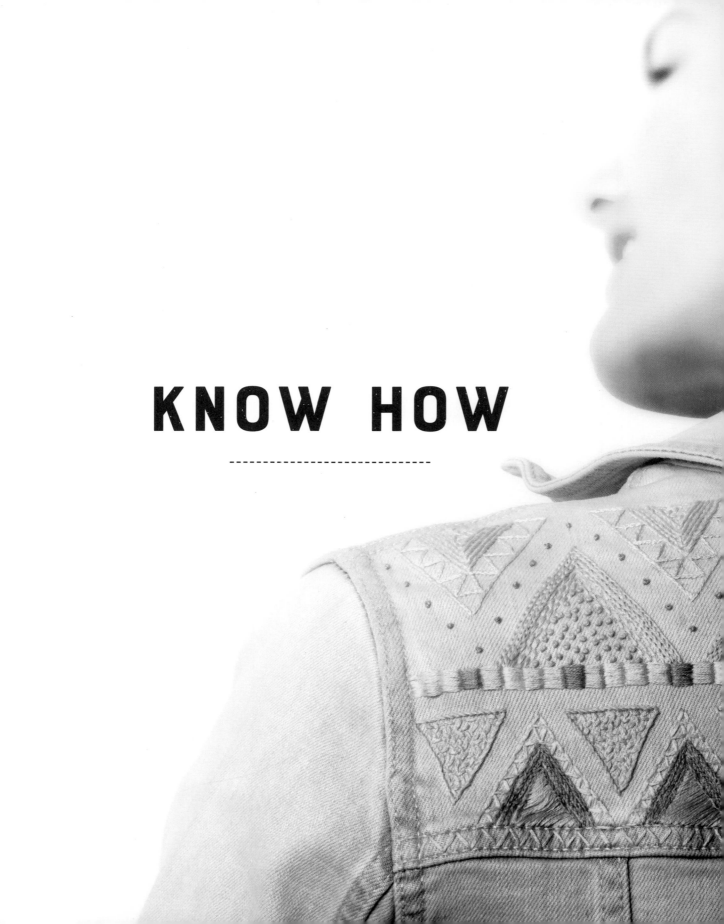

KNOW HOW

EMBROIDERY KIT

Compiling an embroidery kit is a satisfying thing to do! To start, find a nice bag or box that it can all live in. Then gather together a good range of needles, some beautiful threads and the various hard-working essentials that every good embroiderer has to hand; items such as embroidery and fabric scissors, a tape measure and fabric markers suitable for an array of fabrics. Once you have collated the basics, they will last you a long time. You will just need to top up your stash of threads and fabric every now and then.

NEEDLES

There are many different needles available to buy, and it can be confusing knowing which type you need. As a guide, always consider the size of thread and type of fabric you are working with. I have listed below the needles required for the projects in this book, but there are many more out there to choose from for different projects. I recommend having several needles to hand when you are working, as they can easily bend and break.

EMBROIDERY/CREWEL NEEDLES
These needles tend to be relatively short and sharp with a slightly longer eye. This makes them useful for finer fabrics and threads such as stranded cottons. Sizes range from 1–12; the lower the number, the larger the needle.

TAPESTRY NEEDLES
Much larger than embroidery needles and with a bigger eye, tapestry needles are perfect for thicker threads like tapestry wool. The tip of the needle is blunt, allowing it to be used on open canvases and helping avoid splitting fabrics and threads. Sizes range from 13–28; the higher the number, the smaller the needle.

CHENILLE NEEDLES
These needles are the same as a tapestry needle, although the tip is sharp, making them ideal for coarse fabric and thicker threads, such as Perle or tapestry wool. Sizes range from 13–28; the higher the number, the smaller the needle.

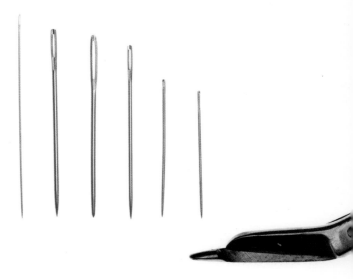

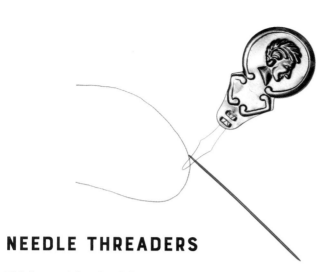

NEEDLE THREADERS

This is a useful tool and there are many options available to purchase, from the basic to the more elaborate. See page 103 for instructions on how to use a basic needle threader.

SCISSORS

EMBROIDERY SCISSORS

Tending to be short and sharp-tipped, embroidery scissors allow you to cut small threads and pieces of fabric with accuracy. There are a variety of blades, such as straight, bent and curved. I find curved are the most useful as they are less likely to rip the fabric if you slip.

FABRIC SCISSORS

These are large, long-bladed scissors specifically for cutting fabric. Make sure you only ever cut fabric with these as they will need sharpening if used for the wrong purpose.

CRAFT SCISSORS

You will need some traditional craft scissors for cutting out paper templates.

HOOPS

Embroidery hoops are usually made from wood and consist of two hoops that screw tightly together, allowing your fabric to be held taut. Sizes range from 3–10in (7.5–25.5cm). There are also hoops available that are attached to stands, allowing you to work with two hands. Be aware that you should never leave fabric in a hoop for too long as it can permanently damage the fabric.

EMBROIDERY STABILIZER

This is needed for embroidering onto finer fabrics and fabric with stretch. It is a synthetic fabric that comes in either black or white and allows fabrics to be worked on under tension without the embroidery distorting. Once the embroidery is complete, any excess fabric can be torn or cut away. There is also a wash-away version available, which is recommended for some of the projects in this book.

PINS

Good-quality stainless steel pins are best with either glass or plastic heads. If any pins become bent or tarnished, dispose of them safely.

MARKERS

ERASABLE PENS

These pens are great for transferring large designs onto fabric, and particularly useful for when there is a chance that the marks may still be visible once the project is finished. Water-soluble pen marks disappear when washed, but can also be removed using a water-spray or dabbing with a wet cotton bud. Air-soluble pen marks disappear in a short period of time; usually within an hour.

CHALK PENS

These non-permanent fine-tipped pens come in a range of colours and can be removed with gentle rubbing. They are not ideal for large designs, as the marks can rub off while you are working the stitching.

WATERPROOF (ARCHIVE) PENS

These fine-tipped pens are useful for permanently marking fabric because they do not run; they are also good for transferring designs onto water-soluble fabric.

BALLPOINT PENS

These pens are needed for transferring designs when using embroidery transfer paper.

PENCIL

Protracting pencils are great for staying sharp and ideal for tracing onto tissue paper.

THIMBLES

There are many types of thimble available to suit different needs. Some people do not like them, but when using a smaller embroidery needle your finger can become sore, and when working with heavy-weight materials they can help you to push the needle through. I prefer thimbles with a metal head and rubber body as these stay on my finger, but you can also get thimbles made entirely of metal or even leather.

RULER AND TAPE MEASURE

A ruler is helpful for plotting out designs and providing crisp edges for you to follow when stitching or cutting out. A tape measure is essential for working with fabric and large-scale projects.

CIRCLE TEMPLATE

A useful tool for creating perfect circles every time; and especially good for denser, non-transparent fabrics when tracing isn't an option.

SET SQUARE

Handy for working projects with sharp, right-angled designs.

TAPESTRY/KNITTING/CROCHET WOOL

These are lovely thick and sturdy yarns, which are perfect for large, bold embroidery designs worked on coarse fabrics.

MACHINE THREAD

Used mainly in this book for tacking stitches, machine thread is fine and can be removed easily without leaving marks on the fabric. Always choose a contrasting colour that shows up well against the fabric you are working on.

METALLIC EMBROIDERY THREAD

There are many metallic embroidery threads available. Care must be taken when using them as they are prone to snapping and twisting.

THREADS

STRANDED COTTON

Probably the most popular of all the embroidery threads, 'skeins' usually come in lengths of 8yd (8m) and consist of six individual threads that can be separated then combined again (see the instructions on page 102). The number of threads needed for the projects in this book are detailed on the relevant pages. When designing your own projects, you can choose the number of threads you would like depending on what suits your design or fabric.

PERLE

A twisted thread with a glossy appearance, Perle comes in a range of thicknesses and is exceptionally durable, making it suitable for many different types of embroidery.

BASIC TECHNIQUES

In addition to learning a variety of stitches (see the Stitch Directory on pages 106–115), there are a few basic techniques that you will need to get to grips with.

TRANSFERRING DESIGNS

To transfer a design onto fabric, there are several methods available to you.

DRAWING AROUND A TEMPLATE

This transfer technique works best for simple shapes on thicker, trickier fabrics or objects.

STEP 1

Photocopy or trace the design onto thin card or thick paper and cut it out to create a template.

STEP 2

Position the template on your chosen fabric and pin it into place. Make sure the pins are at 90 degrees to the template so that it keeps its shape.

STEP 3

Carefully draw around the template with a fabric marker. Always think about what marker is most suitable for your fabric and project (see page 96).

STEP 4

Remove the pins and you are now left with an outline.

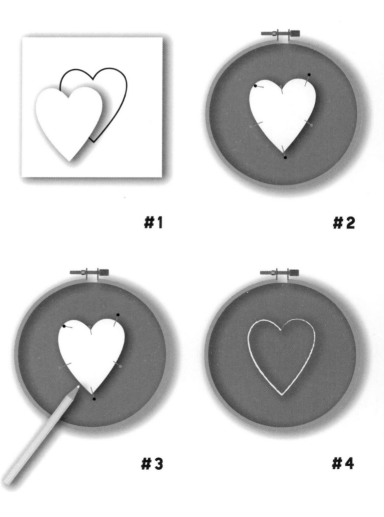

#1   #2

#3   #4

LIGHTBOX/WINDOW METHOD

This method is suitable for finer fabrics. If your fabric is very light in colour, a lightbox may not be necessary.

STEP 1

Photocopy or trace the design onto paper and cut it out. Position it on top of a lightbox and place your chosen fabric on top. If you do not have a lightbox, you can stick the paper and fabric with sticky tape onto a window in daylight.

STEP 2

Using a fabric marker that is suitable for your project and fabric (see page 96), carefully trace over the design.

#1

#2

TACKING OVER TISSUE PAPER

This technique is ideal for thicker fabrics, or fabrics with a bold print. If your design does not have any solid outlines this is also a suitable technique. All tacking stitches should be removed at the end of the project.

STEP 1

Cut out a piece of acid-free tissue paper larger than your design. Place it over your image and trace the outlines with a coloured pencil (do not use a normal pencil as the graphite will mark the thread and fabric).

STEP 2

Decide where on your fabric you want the design to be and pin it into place. Make sure all your pins are tarnish-free.

STEP 3

Using a small embroidery needle (size 10), thread a 16in (40cm) standard length of machine cotton in a contrasting colour to your base fabric. Work a row of tacking (large running stitch) around the inside of your pins. Do not secure this thread tightly as it will eventually be removed.

STEP 4

Remove the pins and work a small tacking stitch over all the outlines of the design. Make sure you keep a longer stitch on top and a smaller stitch on the reverse.

STEP 5

Carefully remove the outer tacking stitches and gently pull away the tissue paper to reveal the design tacked on. If small pieces of tissue paper remain under the stitches they can be removed with tweezers or a tapestry needle. Once your project is complete you can remove all the tacking stitches.

#1

#2

#3

#4

#5

EMBROIDERY TRANSFER PAPER

This type of paper has a coloured powder coating on one side. It is useful for when the design you are working cannot be traced. Use a contrasting colour paper to your base fabric.

STEP 1

Photocopy or trace the design onto paper; then cut out a piece of embroidery transfer paper a little larger than your design. Place the embroidery transfer paper powder side down to your base fabric with the design on top.

#1

STEP 2

With the fabric on a flat, firm surface, draw over the design lines with a ballpoint pen. Be sure to press down firmly and go over the lines several times.

#2

STEP 3

Carefully lift both sheets of paper to reveal a carbon copy of your design. As this is a powder you may want to go over the lines with a suitable fabric marker for your project (see page 96).

#3

✖ Snake Blouse, page 74

EMBROIDERY STABILIZER

This technique requires you to embroider over the stabilizer, then, once the project is complete, remove it by either pulling away or dampening with water. It is therefore not suitable for delicate fabrics, but ideal for tricky, heavy fabrics or items. There are two options available on the market: one is a transparent plastic and the other is an opaque fabric.

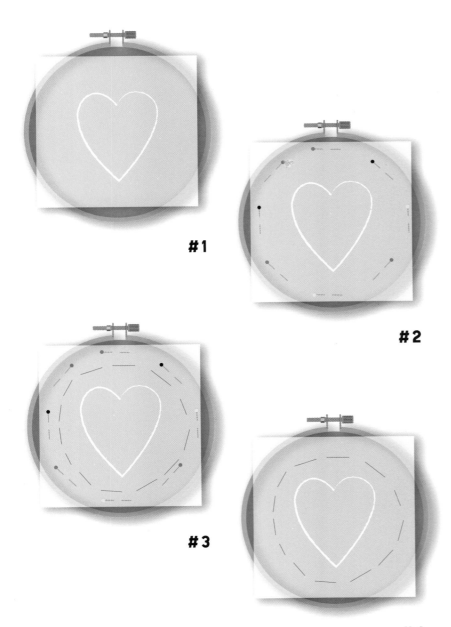

#1

#2

#3

#4

STEP 1

Cut out a piece of water-soluble embroidery stabilizer (transparent or opaque) a little larger than the design. Place it over the image and trace the outlines. If you have used opaque stabilizer, you can trace the outlines with a fabric pen; if you have used transparent stabilizer you will need to use either a gel pen or a waterproof pen in a contrasting colour to your base fabric. Place the stabilizer onto your fabric or item of choice.

STEP 2

Pin the stabilizer into place, positioning the pins well away from the design. Always make sure your pins are sharp and tarnish-free.

STEP 3

Using a small embroidery needle (size 10) and machine thread, work a row of tacking stitches (running stitch) along the inside of the pins. Remove the pins.

Tip

If you are working on a very thick fabric/surface it may be tricky to tack the stabilizer in to place; you can therefore leave out the tacking stitch, but take care when working on your project not to catch your threads or fingers on the pins.

STEP 4

You are now ready to start your embroidery. Once the project is complete, remove the tacking stitch (or pins if using) and gently peel away the stabilizer. If areas remain, simply spray or immerse in water. The stabilizer will disappear in seconds.

SEPARATING STRANDED COTTON

Stranded cotton, used throughout this book, is composed of six strands twisted together so that they look like one thick thread. Often, you will need to use less than six threads in your needle.

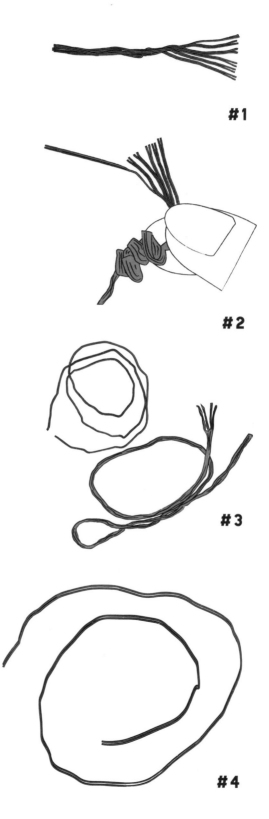

#1

STEP 1

Cut the thread to the required length. Holding the threads at the top, carefully separate one of the six strands.

STEP 2

Holding the single strand, pull upwards while still holding firmly to the top of the other strands (never pull down, as this will tangle the threads). All the embroidery strands will gather up under your fingers.

#2

STEP 3

Always separate one strand at a time, remembering to smooth the remaining strands after ever pull.

STEP 4

Repeat this for as many strands as you need, then put them together.

#3

#4

THREADING A NEEDLE

Trim the threads so there is a clean cut, then pass the thread through the eye of the needle by taking the thread to the needle, not the needle to the thread. This works best with a short tail between your forefinger and thumb.

If you prefer, you can use a needle threader. It is an invaluable bit of kit for threading multiple strands of embroidery thread.

STEP 1
Pick up the needle and push the diamond-shaped wire end of the needle threader through the eye of the needle.

STEP 2
Insert the thread through the diamond shape.

STEP 3
Hold the needle and pull the needle threader; it will bring the thread back through the eye with it.

STEP 4
Your threaded needle is now ready to be used.

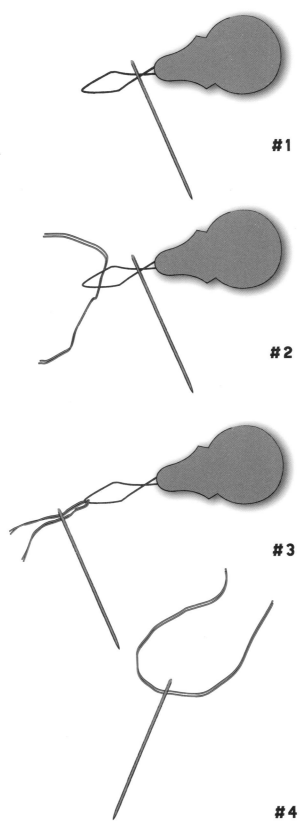

#1

#2

#3

#4

STARTING THREAD

STAB STITCH

Stab stitches are the best way to start a thread, as no loose tails of threads will be left on the reverse of the work. They are intended to be stitched over by the first couple of stitches. Stab stitches should never be visible once your project is complete.

STEP 1

Tie a double knot at the end of your chosen thread and thread your needle. Starting roughly $^3/_8$in (1cm) away from the point you intend to start stitching from, bring the needle down through the fabric, leaving the knot sitting on the front of your work. Bring the needle back up in between the knot and the starting point and make two tiny backstitches (see page 106) with a small gap in between each stitch. Pull the thread firmly with each stitch to ensure it is secure. It is best if the needle pierces the thread trailing underneath, as this makes it extra strong.

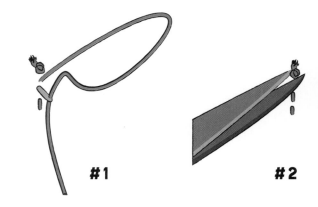

#1 #2

STEP 2

Pull the knot upwards and snip off with embroidery scissors. You can now stitch over the stab stitches with your chosen stitch.

FINISHING THREAD

STAB STITCH

To finish off a thread, work two stab stitches in the same method as above, bringing the thread up to the front of your work and cutting closely to the fabric. These finishing stitches should not be visible, so make sure they are either eventually stitched over by other embroidery or tucked away out of sight.

WEAVING THREAD ON THE REVERSE

If there isn't room for you to finish your thread with stab stitches, the best option is to weave your thread along the reverse of the stitches.

STEP 1

Once you have completed your stitches, pass the needle and thread to the reverse of your work and turn the work over. Carefully weave the thread over and under the stitches by approximately $^3/_8$in (1cm).

STEP 2

Pull the thread gently and snip the tail closely to the stitches with a pair of embroidery scissors, ensuring no tails are left hanging.

Tip

To ensure the thread is extra secure, you can knot the thread onto the reverse stitches as you are weaving, by making a loop and passing the needle through it.

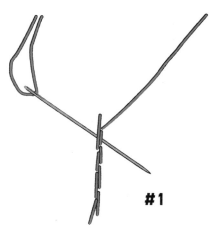

#1

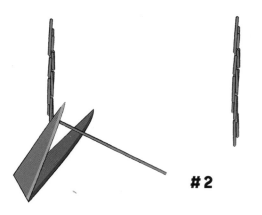

#2

USING AN EMBROIDERY HOOP

An embroidery hoop will keep the fabric taut and secure while you are stitching.

STEP 1

Unscrew the outer piece of the hoop and remove the solid inner ring. Place it onto a solid surface and lay the fabric over it in the centre.

NOTE: The illustration shows the ring on top of the fabric.

STEP 2

Pick up the outer ring and place it on the fabric and ring. Push down on the outer ring to trap the fabric and inner ring.

STEP 3

When the outer ring and inner ring are level, start to tighten the screw. Do not tighten it completely yet; instead, keep it a little loose.

STEP 4

Gently pull on the edges of the fabric to make sure it is taut in the ring. Do not pull too hard or the inner ring will fall out. You are aiming for the fabric to be flat and tight inside the frame. Finally, tighten the screw as far as it will comfortably go.

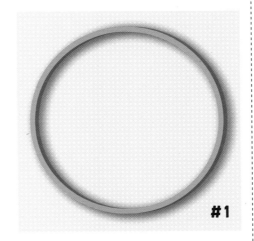

#1

#2

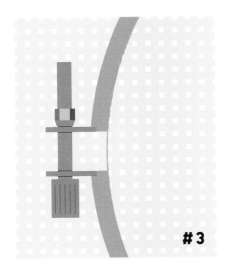

#3

#4

IRONING

You will need a steam iron for pressing several of the projects. Make sure the ironing board cover is clean so that your fabric is not marked during the process. When pressing delicate fabrics, always use a pressing cloth. When pressing an embroidered piece, use a folded towel to create a cushioned bed for the embroidery, then press the embroidered areas on the reverse to avoid flattening the stitches.

STITCH DIRECTORY

Learning different stitches allows you to be creative and imaginative with your embroidery. Here you will find a range of basic and decorative stitches. It is best to grab some spare fabric and practise before you start any of the projects.

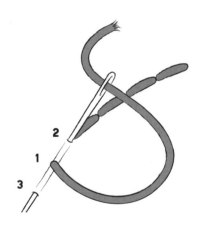

RUNNING STITCH

Working from right to left, bring the needle up to the right side of the work, then back down into the fabric a little way along the stitch line. Bring the needle out again about the same distance along. Repeat this action all along the line.

DOUBLE RUNNING STITCH

When you reach the end of a line of running stitch, go back in the opposite direction, filling in the gaps left between each stitch. This creates a solid line called a double running stitch.

BACKSTITCH

Working from right to left, bring the needle up through the fabric at 1, slightly to the left of the beginning of the line to be worked, then back through at 2, the beginning of the line. Bring the needle up again at 3, a stitch length in front of 1. Repeat the process, going back in again at the starting point, then forward, a stitch length in front.

WHIPPED RUNNING/ BACKSTITCH

Work a line of running stitch or backstitch. Using contrasting thread and a tapestry needle, bring the needle up at one end of the line and pass the needle under each stitch in turn, always in the same direction, without piercing the fabric. When you reach the end of the line, pass the needle back through the fabric into the centre of the last stitch.

SPLIT STITCH

STEP 1
Working from left to right, bring the needle up at 1, the beginning of the line to be worked, then down at 2, a stitch length to the right.

STEP 2
Pull the thread through to form the first stitch, then bring the needle up through the centre of the stitch, 3, so that it is split.

STEP 3
Take the needle back through the fabric a stitch length in front. Repeat along the length of the line.

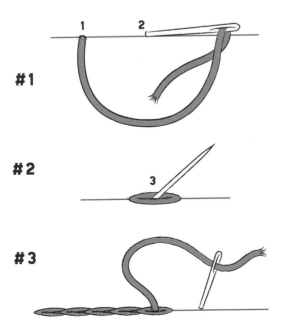

STEM STITCH

STEP 1
Working from left to right, bring the needle up at 1, at the beginning of the line to be worked, then down a stitch length to the right, at 2, just below the line. Pull the thread through to form the first stitch, then bring the needle up slightly above the centre of the first stitch at 3, and along the line to the right at 4, another stitch length along.

STEP 2
Repeat the process along the length of the line. You can vary the length of the stitches and the angle, to make a thinner or thicker line.

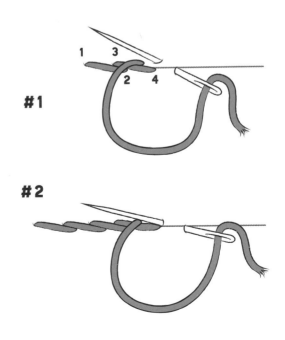

CHAIN STITCH

STEP 1

Working from top to bottom (as shown), bottom to top, or right to left, whichever you prefer, bring the needle up at 1, at the beginning of the line to be worked, then back down at the same point and out again at 2, a stitch length along the line, with the tip of the needle over the loop of thread.

STEP 2

Pull the thread through to form the first stitch, 1. Take the needle down through the loop at 2 and out again at 3, a stitch length along the line, with the tip of the needle over the loop of thread once again.

STEP 3

Repeat along the length of the line to create a chain of linked loops.

STEP 4

To finish off the line, secure the last loop of the chain with a short stitch, taking the needle to the back of the work. Fasten off.

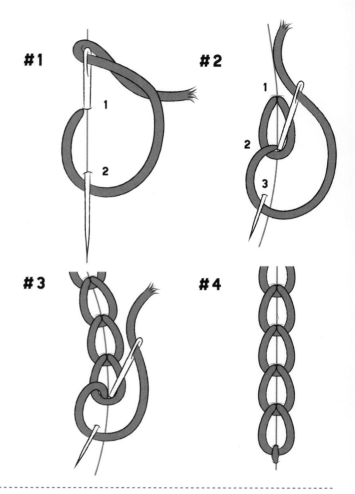

DETACHED CHAIN STITCH (LAZY DAISY)

Once you can create a line of linked chain stitches, you can easily work individual stitches that can be used in many ways, including for flower petals; hence detached chain stitch also being known as 'lazy daisy'.

Cherries Beach Bag, page 50

CROSS STITCH

The Astro Cap on page 58 uses a basic cross stitch composed of two crossed running stitches. More detailed cross-stitch work can be done on aida fabric by following the instructions below.

STEP 1

Secure your thread, then make a diagonal stitch. Trap the tail end on the reverse of the fabric. If this first diagonal stitch went from top left to bottom right, then continue to always go top left to bottom right. This will ensure every stitch is identical. Bring the needle through the fabric from the back and go through the hole in the next row at a diagonal.

STEP 2

If you are making a row of the same colour stitches then do the first diagonal stitch all the way along the row first.

STEP 3

Keep checking the reverse to ensure the tail end is trapped.

STEP 4

To complete the cross shape, stitch back along the row of diagonal stitches in the opposite direction.

STEP 5

To step down to the next row, bring the needle through the hole that's one across from the last hole it went through. This will enable you to make a diagonal stitch following the same pattern as the row above. Note that the first stitch in the row will be back to front as you will be bringing the needle through the hole that is at the bottom of the stitch.

STEP 6

Bring the needle up to the hole that is on a diagonal to the hole the thread is exiting from. Follow the same direction as the rest of your stitches. Continue to stitch in the same way as you did for the rows above. When you have finished, secure your thread and cut off any excess.

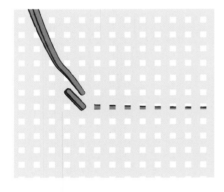

#1

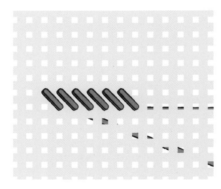

#2

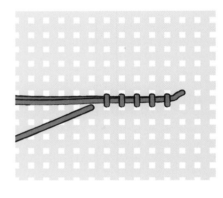

#3

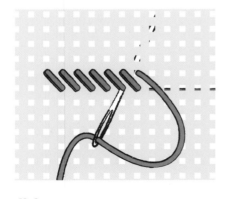

#4

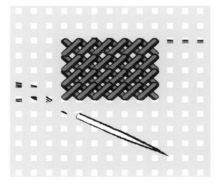

#5

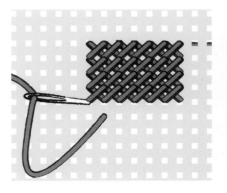

#6

TRELLIS STITCH

STEP 1
Start your thread on the design line. Starting in the middle of the shape, bring the needle up on the outer line and bring down on the opposite side, depending on the desired angle.

STEP 2
Pull the thread so that it lies flat and bring the needle up farther along the design, then take the thread down on the opposite side. Make sure the lines are parallel.

STEP 3
Continue working lines in the same direction. Then working from the middle, work the lines in the opposite direction.

STEP 4
Start again from the middle and work the lines at 90 degrees to the previous lines.

STEP 5
Work the other side in the same way and finish off your thread again on the design line.

STEP 6
Change threads and work small cross stitches from one side to the other over the crossover points of the trellis. Ensure the crosses are worked in the same order.

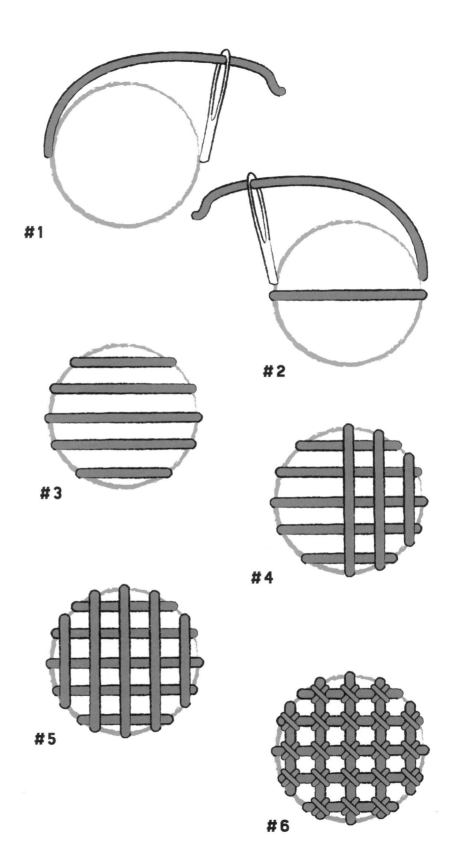

#1

#2

#3

#4

#5

#6

SATIN STITCH

Satin stitches should be worked parallel and close together. It is recommended to work a tight row of split stitch first and work the satin stitch over this, without any gaps between them, to create a smooth edge. The stitches should be quite short, so that they do not snag or pull; therefore, it is best that the shapes to be filled are fairly small.

STEP 1
Always start in the centre of the shape to keep the angle of the stitches the same.

STEP 2
Work one half of the shape.

STEP 3
Return to the centre to work the second half.

#1

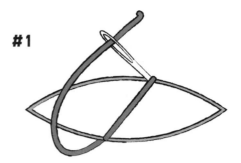

#2

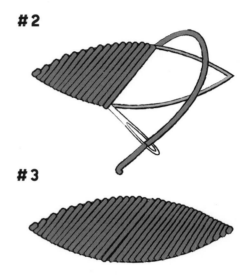

#3

PADDED SATIN STITCH

For a raised effect, pad out the shape to be filled by building up layers of satin stitch.

✖ French-bulldog Hoop, page 86

LAID STITCH

STEP 1
Always start in the centre of the shape and work outwards. Bring the needle up on the line of the shape you want to fill. Take it down directly opposite.

STEP 2
Pull the thread down through the hole and bring the needle up directly adjacent.

STEP 3
Take the thread back down directly opposite, next to where you first brought the needle up.

STEP 4
Draw the thread through to create a parallel stitch, then continue to work parallel stitches up and down across the shape.

STEP 5
Once the shape is filled, secure the thread to finish.

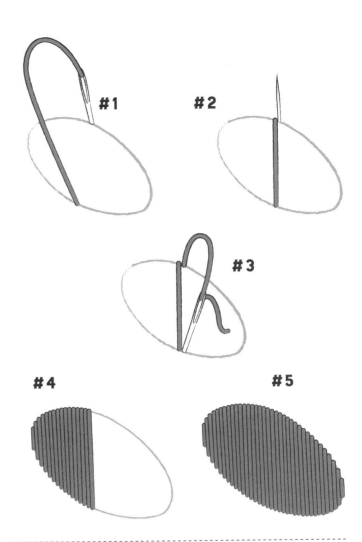

✖ Aztec Denim Jacket, page 36

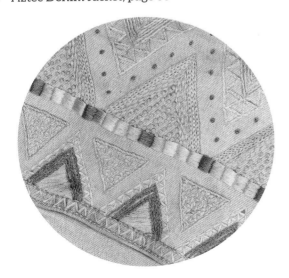

SEED STITCH

Seeding is simply worked in small, individual running stitches. Stitches should be worked at the same length, keeping the angles constantly varied.

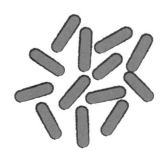

LONG-AND-SHORT STITCH

For larger shapes, use long-and-short stitch, a variation of satin stitch.

STEP 1

Always work a tight row of split stitch around any outer edge. Work the first row in alternating long-and-short stitches, with the stitches going over and under the split stitch. Stitches should be no longer than $^3/_8$in (1cm) and no shorter than $^{13}/_{64}$in (5mm). Keep the lengths varied and not in a regimented order – this will avoid creating a 'lump' under the next row.

STEP 2

For the next row, bring the needle up from the reverse, making sure to pierce the stitches of the previous row. Stitches can be kept the same length from now on ($^3/_8$in/1cm). Work the stitches closely together and in a random formation to create a natural effect.

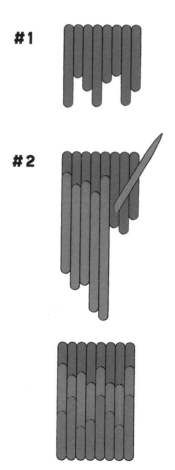

#1

#2

FLY STITCH

Fly stitch is a looped stitch that can be used to suggest flying birds. You can easily vary the size of the stitch and the length of the straight stitch that holds down the loop. It can also be extended into vertical lines of stitches, as for the Palm-tree Tee (see below).

Bring the thread up through the fabric at 1 and hold it down with your thumb or finger; take the needle back through the fabric a small distance away at 2, then back up between the two points and a little way down at 3. Make sure the loop of thread is under the tip of the needle and pull the thread through, then take the needle back into the fabric slightly below at 4 to complete the stitch. Take the needle up through the fabric where you want the next stitch to be.

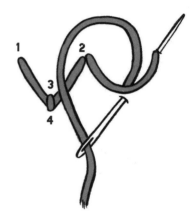

✖ Palm-tree Tee, page 46

FRENCH KNOT

STEP 1
Bring the needle up and hold the thread taught with finger and thumb.

STEP 2
Wind once (or a maximum of twice) around the needle. Don't let go of the thread!

STEP 3
Still holding tightly to the thread, insert the needle very closely to where the thread started. Pull the needle through to the reverse while continuing to hold onto the thread. At the last moment, release the thread as the needle goes completely through to the back.

COUCHING

STEP 1
Bring the thread to be couched up through the fabric at the beginning of the line. As long as it isn't too thick, you can do this by threading it into a large-eyed needle. This example shows a double row of threads. Thread the needle with a finer thread and make several small upright stitches along the thicker one, to hold it securely in place.

STEP 2
To make a second line alongside the first, when you get to the end of the first line, bend the thread to be couched back. Take a small stitch across the point where it folds, then work a second line of couching using small, straight stitches, as before.

STEP 3
To make a loop, or to outline a shape, take the thread in the direction you wish, making small couching stitches to hold it in place as you go. In this example, the couching stitches are angled, rather than straight.

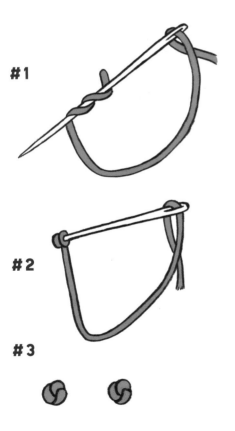

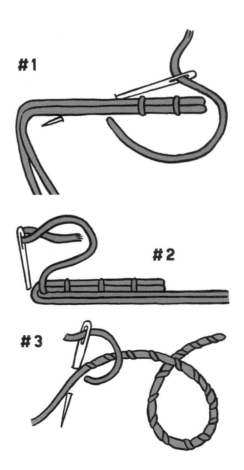

TEMPLATES

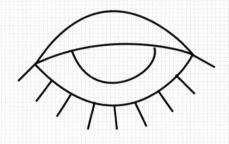 

EYES

Copy at 100%
(see page 8)

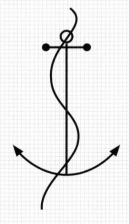

ANCHOR

Copy at 100%
(see page 12)

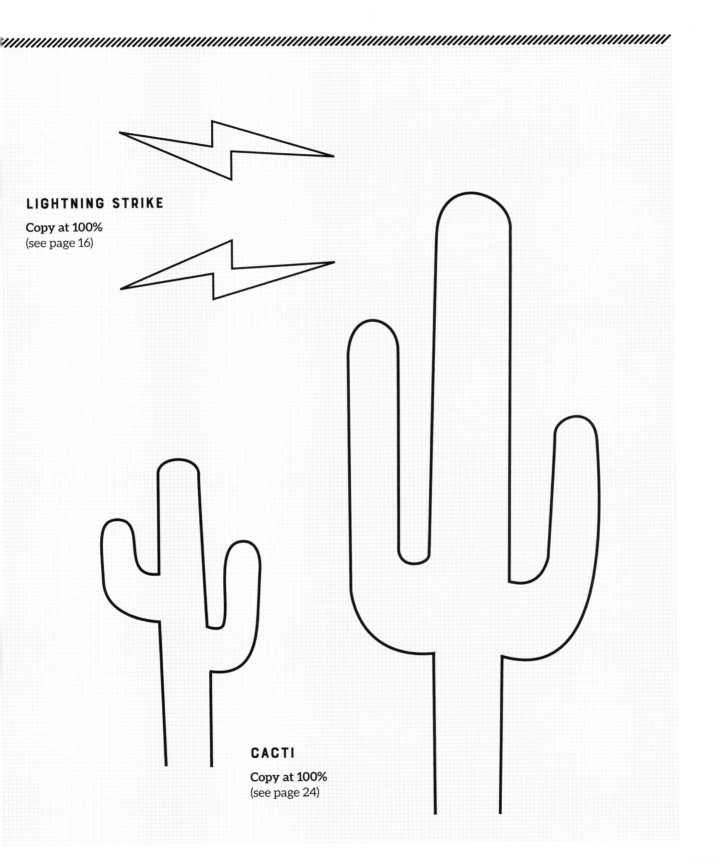

LIGHTNING STRIKE

Copy at 100%
(see page 16)

CACTI

Copy at 100%
(see page 24)

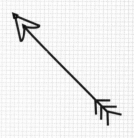

MEXICAN SKULL

Copy at 100%
(see page 28)

LOVE HEART

Copy at 100%
(see page 32)

AZTEC

Copy at 230%
(see page 36)

MONSTERA

Copy at 195%
(see page 42)

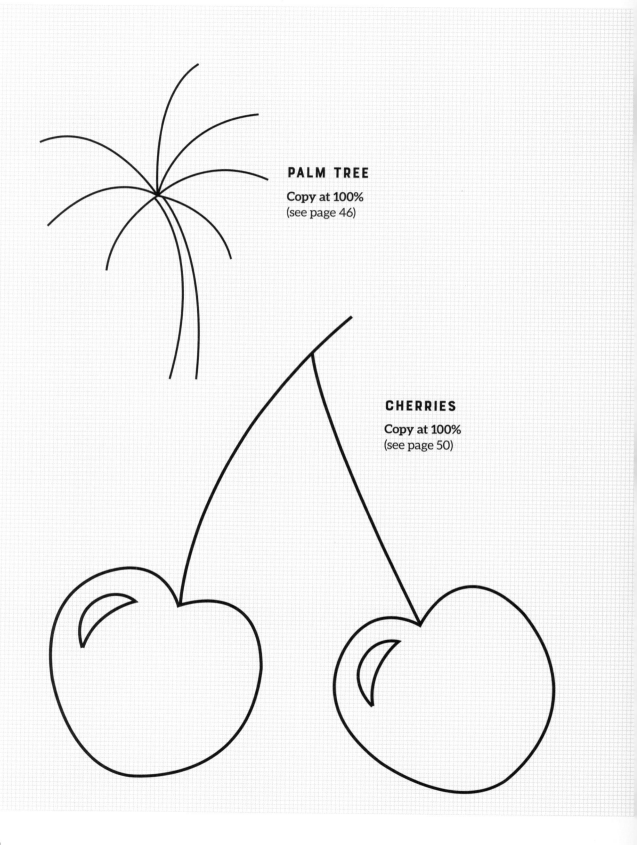

PALM TREE

Copy at 100%
(see page 46)

CHERRIES

Copy at 100%
(see page 50)

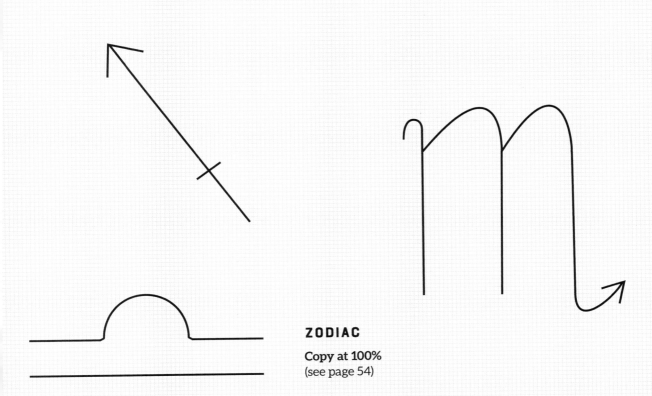

ZODIAC

Copy at 100%
(see page 54)

ASTRO

Copy at 100%
(see page 58)

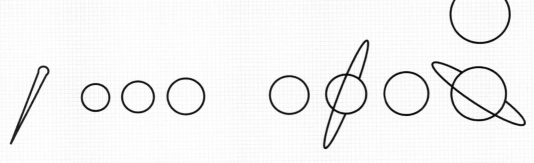

PINEAPPLE

Copy at 100%
(see page 62)

LIPS

Copy at 100%
(see page 66)

SUN & WAVES

Copy at 280%
(see page 70)

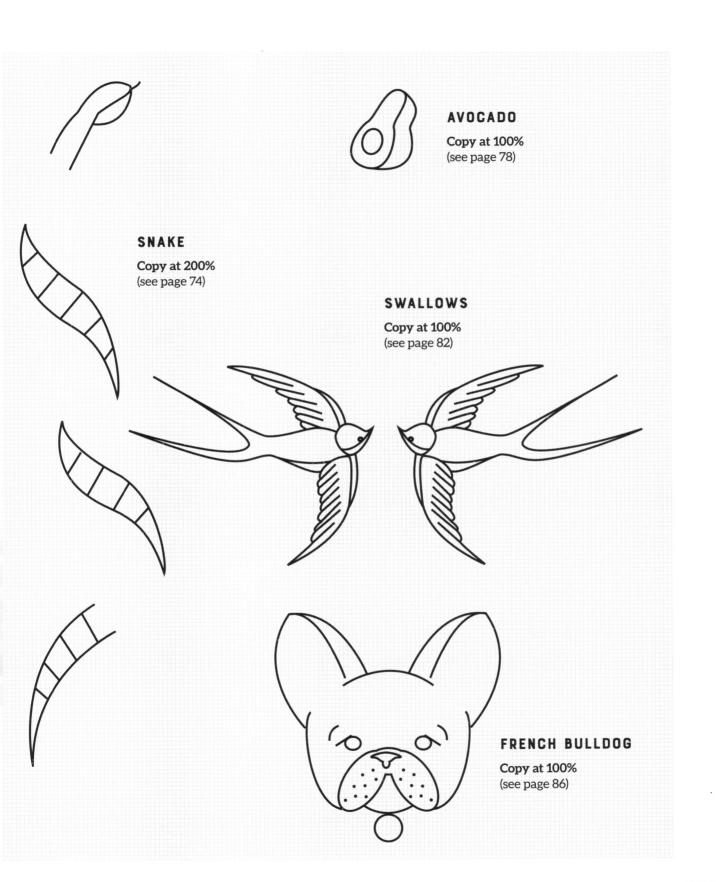

AVOCADO

Copy at 100%
(see page 78)

SNAKE

Copy at 200%
(see page 74)

SWALLOWS

Copy at 100%
(see page 82)

FRENCH BULLDOG

Copy at 100%
(see page 86)

RESOURCES

UK

Anchor
www.anchorcrafts.com

D.M.C.
www.dmc.com

John James Needles
www.jjneedles.com

John Lewis
www.johnlewis.com

Lakeside Needlecrafts
www.lakesideneedlecraft.com

Royal School of Needlework
www.royal-needlework.org.uk

USA

Jo-ann Stores
www.joann.com

Kai Scissors
www.kaiscissors.com

Michaels
www.michaels.com

ABOUT THE AUTHOR

Amy Burt, aka 'Lady B Embroidery', is an embroidery artist and tutor. Amy was introduced to hand sewing by her Granny as a child, but it wasn't until she moved to Berlin, Germany, in her early 20s that she rediscovered her childhood passion and began to make and sell handmade leathercraft goods.

After returning to the UK in 2014, Amy trained as a tutor at the Royal School of Needlework at Hampton Court Palace, London. There are fewer than 40 RSN tutors around the world. She is qualified to teach over 25 different embroidery techniques.

Amy takes great pride in being one of just two tutors teaching 'Technical Hand Embroidery' for the RSN's Bachelor of Arts (Hons) Degree in Hand Embroidery, partnered with the University of Creative Arts. As well as teaching for the RSN, Amy regularly gives private lessons at her home studio in East London, and often travels around the world to teach.

Amy also works as a freelance embroiderer in the British fashion industry. She frequently stitches for Alexander McQueen, and worked for many years as a Senior Embroiderer at the British Haute Couture fashion house Ralph & Russo.

Her personal work includes private commissions for collectors and independent fashion designers. In 2018, her embroidery of 'The Young Stevie Nicks' was chosen from over 20,000 pieces of art to be displayed in the Royal Academy of Arts 250th Summer Exhibition.

Amy lives in Hackney, East London, with her little dog Gertie.
www.ladybembroidery.co.uk

ACKNOWLEDGEMENTS

I would like to thank:

My Mum and my late Dad, who have always supported me with my many careers and sometimes unique life choices! I hope I make you proud.

The Degree Team at the RSN, who have always made me feel welcome and continue to put their trust in me. I am very proud to be part of this team.

Joe Piper and Athena, for lending me the camera equipment to create this book.

My RSN colleagues, especially Marg Dier and Lisa Bilby, for their never-ending advice and support.

GMC Publications, for asking me to write this book.

All of my current and former students, who forever amaze and inspire me.

Lastly, I would like to thank my friends that are spread around the world, who have had to listen to me worry about stitch choices and designs! Thank you to those who have stuck by me all these years, especially Chunk.

I dedicate this book to the memory of my Dad x

INDEX

To order a book, contact:

GMC Publications Ltd
Castle Place, 166 High Street,
Lewes, East Sussex,
BN7 1XU
United Kingdom
Tel: +44 (0)1273 488005
www.gmcbooks.com

First published 2021 by
Guild of Master Craftsman Publications Ltd
Castle Place, 166 High Street, Lewes,
East Sussex, BN7 1XU

Text © Amy Burt, 2021 Copyright in the Work
© GMC Publications Ltd, 2021

ISBN 978 1 78494 587 9

A catalogue record for this book is available from the
British Library.

PUBLISHER Jonathan Bailey
PRODUCTION MANAGER Jim Bulley
COMMISSIONING & SENIOR PROJECT EDITOR Dominique Page
DESIGN & ART DIRECTION Wayne Blades
PHOTOGRAPHERS Neil Grundy & Amy Burt
ILLUSTRATOR Robin Shields

Additional images by Shutterstock.com
Colour origination by GMC Reprographics
Printed and bound in China